gene and sacrifice

the report of the Clergy Stipends Review Group

GS 1408

CHURCH HOUSE
PUBLISHING

Church House Publishing
Church House,
Great Smith Street,
London SW1P 3NZ

ISBN 0 7151 2603 2

Published 2001 for the Ministry
Division of the Archbishops'
Council by Church House
Publishing

Typeset in 9pt Franklin Gothic

Cover design by Visible Edge

Printed by Creative Print and
Design Group, Ebbw Vale, Wales

*This report has only the authority of
the Group that produced it.*

contents

contents

preface

The clergy of the Church of England are crucial people in the task of sharing the gospel of Jesus Christ in the nation. They minister in and to a wide variety of communities with public worship, pastoral care, evangelism and social concern. The shape of ministry will indeed change over the coming years as the Church responds to the changing needs of the community and the challenges of sharing the good news of Jesus. It is essential that our key leaders are well trained, adequately resourced and properly remunerated for our shared tasks of ministry. This report is simply one contribution to this wider picture.

In 1999 the Archbishops' Council set up a group to review the stipends paid to clergy and licensed lay workers. The most important reason for this was to assess whether stipends were adequate to prevent clergy from suffering financial hardship. Reports from a number of sources suggested that households with children where the stipend was the only source of income were particularly hard pressed. There was also concern about the question of stipend coherence across the Church of England, whilst recognizing also the need for local flexibility, not least because of issues of clergy mobility and deployment.

The Review Group met 16 times between September 1999 and June 2001. It believed strongly that its deliberations should take place within a biblical and theological context. One of the questions which occupied the Group was the nature of the obligation that the Church has to those who respond to God's call to minister on behalf of the whole people of God. Many who seek ordination willingly forego secure, perhaps prosperous, financial futures. Certainly they experience a considerable loss of privacy, which is rarely comprehended by lay people. They have increasingly to juggle scarce resources of people and finance and are called on to make public witness to a faith that is, for many, increasingly a matter of indifference. The Group concluded that a generous, even sacrificial, financial response is required from lay people towards the support of those who have themselves sacrificed much.

This report offers a new definition for the stipend and recommends a benchmark to be used in determining the level of stipends. It recognizes the need for a more professional approach to conditions of service. It recommends a significant increase in the levels of stipend paid to both assistant staff and clergy of incumbent status. It also proposes a new way of estimating the value of the housing component of the remuneration package; a new way of computing the higher stipends paid to senior clergy; a new and more flexible stipends structure for clergy of incumbent status; and a scheme to assist clergy with house purchase earlier in their ministry than is currently allowed under the retirement housing scheme.

I should like to thank all those people who have contributed to the work. Some are listed in the report but many others, whose contribution is not recorded explicitly, gave advice. The support of all these people has been greatly welcomed.

The lion's share of thanks must go to the members of the Review Group. They have given unstintingly of their time and abilities, with patience, good humour and deep commitment to the task at hand. Most of the time there has been unanimity about the recommendations. On occasions there have been points of disagreement that are made clear in the text but these have been discussed in a spirit of deep respect for opposing viewpoints.

Our assessors have provided both technical advice and wise counsel during our discussions. My thanks are due to them also. The staff have been bedrocks of support. They have been committed to this task beyond the call of duty. They have responded to the many requests made upon them, shared with the assessors and group members the job of drafting the report, and managed the process of refining the text and preparing it for the publishing department. They have also been greatly supportive of me in my role as Chairman. Margaret Jeffery (secretary to the group), Patrick Shorrock, Stewart Harper, Jim Smith and Jackie Freestone deserve our grateful thanks.

This report is an important contribution to the shape of the ministry of the Church of England in the future. It does not speak into a vacuum. There are many challenges facing the Church, not least financial ones. The group has been careful to spell out a hierarchy of its aspirations, recognizing that the radical nature of these proposals are likely to need to be implemented in stages. However, my own experience is that the proper financial remuneration of the clergy is ranked by the faithful members of our congregations as the principal priority to which the church should direct its resources.

The Revd Dr Richard Turnbull
Chairman, Clergy Stipends Review Group
September 2001

membership and terms of reference

the membership of the Review Group

The Revd Canon Lesley Bentley (Member of the Deployment, Remuneration and Conditions of Service Committee)

Mr Alan King* (Chairman, Diocesan Board of Finance, Bath and Wells. Member of the Finance Committee and the Deployment, Remuneration and Conditions of Service Committee)

The Ven. Dr John Marsh, Archdeacon of Blackburn* (Chairman until May 2001)

Ms Hilary Oliver (Financial Consultant, Ernst & Young)

Mr David Phillips (Diocesan Secretary, Chelmsford. Member of the Deployment, Remuneration and Conditions of Service Committee)

The Ven. Robert Reiss*, Archdeacon of Surrey

Canon Bryan Sandford* (Member of the Finance Committee and the Deployment, Remuneration and Conditions of Service Committee)

Mr Keith Stevens (Former Director of Group Personnel, Lloyds TSB. Member of the Deployment, Remuneration and Conditions of Service Committee)

The Revd Dr Richard Turnbull* (Chairman from May 2001. Member of the Finance Committee)

assessors

Mr Christopher Daws (Financial and Deputy Secretary, Church Commissioners)

Mr Shaun Farrell (Financial Secretary, Archbishops' Council)

The Ven. Dr Gordon Kuhrt (Director, Ministry Division, Archbishops' Council)

Mr Roger Radford (Secretary, Church of England Pensions Board)

the terms of reference

(i) To consider the concept and definition of the stipend;

(ii) To examine the content of the clergy remuneration package (including retirement provision) and its comparability with remuneration for other groups;

*denotes membership of General Synod

(iii) To ascertain, through a properly conducted large-scale survey of clergy and consultations with dioceses and charities, the financial circumstances of clergy;

(iv) To review the size of dignitaries' differentials;

(v) In conjunction with the Finance Committee, to evaluate the affordability and long-term financial sustainability of the present arrangements and any proposals for change;

(vi) To consider the implications of any proposals for:

clergy deployment and partnership between dioceses;

future numbers of stipendiary clergy and patterns of ministry;

(vii) To consider whether the present structure for setting stipends should be retained and outline possible alternative structures;

(viii) To consult with the Church Commissioners, the Pensions Board and dioceses;

(ix) To consult with other national church bodies through the Churches Main Committee and government agencies on matters of fiscal and taxation policy which affect stipends, in particular the treatment of benefits in kind;

(x) To determine options for wide debate within the Church.

a summary of the recommendations of the clergy stipends review group

chapter 2   the remuneration of the clergy

1   We recommend the retention of the concept of stipend, but modified in understanding and definition (paragraph 2.79).

2   We recommend that the following definition of stipend given below (paragraph 2.81) be adopted.

'The stipend is part of the remuneration package that is paid for the exercise of office. It reflects the level of responsibility held. This package acknowledges the dual demands in Scripture of generosity and sacrifice on both those who receive the stipend and those who raise the necessary funds.'

3   We recommend that two principles should govern the adoption of the definition of the stipend (paragraphs 2.82 and 2.83).

Firstly, that the principle adopted is that of 'remuneration for the exercise of office' rather than a 'maintenance allowance'. This has a number of implications:

- The principle of differentials for responsibility is allowed for;
- Subsistence levels of pay are not allowed for;
- Pay should be related to posts, not households or personal circumstances;
- Circumstantial maintenance payments (e.g. child allowances) are not allowed for.

The second guiding principle is that of 'generosity and sacrifice'. This would suggest the following implications:

- Clergy remuneration should represent a primary call on the budgets of the church, national, diocesan and parochial;

- The reasonable expectation of the clergy that any comparisons made are with professional secular groups does not in itself imply that comparable remuneration should be paid;

- Differentials, where paid, should be modest.

chapter 3   the level of the stipend

4   **We recommend that the National Minimum Stipend should be the minimum stipend for all clergy and licensed lay workers holding full-time appointments (paragraph 3.13).**

5   **We recommend that there should be an increase in the National Stipend Benchmark for incumbents from 1.05 of the National Minimum Stipend (as at present) to 1.1 of the National Minimum Stipend (paragraph 3.14).**

6   **We recommend that additional payments for children should not be made (paragraph 3.20).**

7   **We recommend that additional payments should not be made to take into account the additional costs associated with living in rural areas (paragraph 3.22).**

8   **We recommend that full-time or part-time stipendiary clergy should receive the appropriate stipend for the post they occupy irrespective of whether their spouse is also stipendiary (paragraph 3.26)**

9   **We recommend that the Central Stipends Authority bases its estimate of the value of the housing component of the remuneration package on the costs of purchasing a detached house. This should be discounted by 25% to reflect the disadvantages of living in provided accommodation (paragraph 3.45).**

10   **We recommend that the appropriate level for an incumbent's remuneration (that is, stipend and housing) should be approximately 80% of the starting salary of a head teacher of a large primary school (paragraph 3.54).** On 2001/02 figures, our recommendation is a minimum of £20,000.

chapter 4   the concept and level of differentials

11   We believe that some modest differentials in clergy pay are both theologically reasonable and generally acceptable in the Church of England (paragraph 4.18).

12   We recommend that the ratios between differentials in the Church should be simplified as follows (paragraph 4.34).

	Current stipend (multiple of National Minimum Stipend)	New differential
Residentiary Canon	1.30	–
Archdeacon	1.58	**1.6**
Dean/Suffragan Bishop	1.59	**1.7**
Diocesan Bishop	1.94	**2**
Bishop of London	2.92	**3**
Archbishop of York	3.13	**3.25**
Archbishop of Canterbury	3.57	**3.75**

chapter 5   a new stipends system

13   We recommend that a new stipends system should be adopted. It should have the following features (paragraph 5.7):

(i)   **All of the Central Stipends Authority's recommendations should be expressed as multiples of the National Minimum Stipend (NMS).**

(ii)   **There should be an Incumbent's Stipend Guideline (ISG). This should be set at 1.1 of the NMS, rather than the 1.05 of the NMS at which the National Stipend Benchmark is currently set.**

(iii)   **The CSA should offer guidance about regional adjustments for the ISG.**

(iv)   **In order to allow dioceses some flexibility, including differential payments to a limited number of their clergy, the CSA recommendations should specify a ceiling below which at least 80% of clergy in the diocese should be paid.**

(v)   **There should be a further ceiling for all clergy of incumbent status, which would act as a maximum stipend. The flexibility might permit incumbents to be paid in the range (i) £20,000 – £21,800 regionally adjusted or (ii) £20,000 – £23,600 unadjusted, depending on the model adopted.**

14   The Group was not able to agree on the level of these ceilings in relation to the National Minimum Stipend. It was also not able to agree on whether figures for incumbent's stipends should be regionalised. The arguments for and against are set out in paragraphs 5.10ff. **We recommend that these issues be debated widely in the Church in the hope that a national consensus may be achieved (paragraph 5.19).**

chapter 6   the process of setting stipends

15   **We recommend that the CSA should continue to make national recommendations about stipend levels, and carry out its functions by liaising with dioceses and the Church Commissioners (paragraph 6.16).**

16   **We recommend that each diocese should have a committee with responsibility for setting remuneration policy in that diocese (paragraph 6.24).**

17   **We make recommendations concerning the status and membership of such a committee (paragraph 6.25).**

18   **We recommend that diocesan remuneration policies would need to cover the following areas (paragraph 6.27):**

- **what allowance the diocese makes for regional variations in the cost of living;**
- **which posts should carry a differential and how much;**
- **whether the differential is given for a defined period and the reason for it;**
- **how the ceilings for differential payments for clergy of incumbent status are applied within the diocese.**

19   **We recommend that each Diocesan Remuneration Policy should be published within the diocese following approval by the diocesan synod and in the CSA's annual report to the General Synod (paragraph 6.27).**

20   **We recommend that clergy should be represented on these Remuneration Committees, subject to clarification between the Legal Advisory Commission and the Charity Commissioners (paragraph 6.28).**

chapter 7   housing

21   We recommend that the Church of England continues to provide housing for clergy as part of their remuneration package (paragraph 7.23).

22   We recommend that every diocese should have in place policies relating to the standards of accommodation and the mutual expectations of the clergy and the diocese in respect of any work to be done to the house, have them approved by their diocesan synod or other appropriate body, and communicate them widely to the clergy and parishes (paragraph 7.26).

23   We recommend, similarly, that policies in respect of the standards of assistant staff accommodation should be published widely so that there is clarity between all parties involved (paragraph 7.27).

24   We recommend that clergy should not be asked to assume responsibility for paying water charges (paragraph 7.29). Although there would be more to be gained in terms of clarity and accountability for clergy to bear these costs, such a change would not be tax-efficient.

25   We recommend that further work to simplify the Church's legal systems in regard to housing be undertaken at an early date by dioceses, the Archbishops' Council and Church Commissioners (paragraph 7.31).

chapter 8   pensions

26   We recommend that there should be no changes in the current pension differentials (paragraph 8.38).

27   We recommend that the Pensions Board, the Church Commissioners, dioceses and clergy charities consider the possibility of finding sufficient capital for loans to provide the 'pump priming' for the purpose of providing capital to assist clergy to enter the housing market (paragraph 8.44).

chapter 9   other issues

28   We recommend that the General Synod's Method of Computing Income should be retained (paragraph 9.16).

29 We recommend to clergy charities that the invaluable help they provide for clergy might be focused on the following (paragraph 9.21):

   (i) reconsidering their investment policies to make loans to clergy to assist them in entering the housing market;

   (ii) providing assistance for clergy with children, particularly with a non-earning spouse or no spouse;

   (iii) assistance with paying off higher education tuition fees and student loans.

chapter 10   affordability

30 We recommend the following hierarchy of aspirations (paragraph 10.18):

   (i) to bring stipends for assistant staff (including licensed lay workers) up to the National Minimum Stipend;

   (ii) to increase the National Stipend Benchmark from its current level of 1.05 of the National Minimum Stipend to 1.1 of the National Minimum Stipend;

   (iii) to introduce an Incumbents' Stipend Guideline, equivalent, with housing included, to approximately 80% of the starting salary of the head teacher of a large primary school;

   (iv) to adopt a stipends structure as described in Chapter 5.

glossary and
list of abbreviations

AEI	Average Earnings Index
CSA	Central Stipends Authority
DBF	Diocesan Board of Finance
DRACSC	Deployment, Remuneration and Conditions of Service Committee of the Archbishops' Council
DSF	Diocesan Stipends Fund
'Green Guide'	*Parsonages: A Design Guide* (Church Commissioners, 1998)
HLC	Heating, Lighting and Cleaning allowance. Part of the stipend can be paid tax free as reimbursement for the expenses of heating, lighting and cleaning the official house. It is not a payment in addition to stipend, but rather part of the stipend reclassified as tax-free
Inter Diocesan Finance Forum	A body, made up of representatives from each diocese and from the central church bodies, which meets twice a year to discuss the financial issues affecting the church
ISG	Incumbent's Stipend Guideline
Lichfield Scale	The scale on which principals and lecturers at theological colleges and courses are paid
MSF	Manufacturing, Science and Finance Union
NMS	National Minimum Stipend. The level below which no full-time clergy of incumbent status should be paid
NSB	National Stipend Benchmark
RPI	Retail Price Index
RSB	Regional Stipend Benchmark. The NSB adjusted for each diocese to take account of regional differences in the cost of living
Working as One Body	*The Report of the Archbishops' Commission on the Organisation of the Church of England* (CHP, 1995)

chapter 1
introduction

the background to the review

1.1 In 1967 *Partners in Ministry*, the Fenton Morley Report on the Deployment and Payment of the Clergy, advocated that the remuneration of the clergy should be based on certain principles. These were as follows.

'1) It (the system of clergy remuneration) should be flexible enough to enable the Church to pay its clergy and lay workers in the places and positions where they can be best deployed. Deployment and payment ... cannot be separated the one from the other.

2) It should provide the highest possible degree of uniformity in the payment given in similar situations, both within dioceses and between one diocese and another.

3) It should not impede by financial uncertainty the mobility of the clergy, in particular their movement to the right post at the right time whether in the same or another diocese ...

4) It should relieve every clergyman of financial anxiety and enable him to discharge his duties to his family ...

5) It must be accepted by the laity as fair and be so designed to stimulate and attract voluntary giving.'

1.2 The principle of stipend uniformity has thus been accepted by the Church of England for many years. Uniformity has never meant, however, that all stipends have been absolutely equal and acceptance of stipend uniformity has always been combined with an element of diocesan flexibility.

1.3 In 1995 the Church Commissioners as the Central Stipends Authority set up a working group to test whether dioceses still favoured the principle of stipend uniformity. This was in response to concerns from some dioceses that there was too much divergence in stipend levels and concerns from others that central recommendations did not take account of the greater living costs in London and the South East. There were further questions about how uniformity should be defined and the mechanisms that might be put in place to maintain it. The working group was chaired by Mr John Leigh, then Chairman of the Blackburn Diocesan Board of Finance, and included members from the dioceses of Guildford, Lincoln and Sheffield.

1.4 The consultations undertaken by the working party confirmed that dioceses were still broadly in favour of the principle of uniformity for reasons of equity and clergy mobility. It was agreed that there ought to be a small amount of diocesan flexibility built around a centrally recommended stipend. It was also agreed for the first time that stipends should reflect regional variations in the cost of living. Conformity within this system would be maintained by peer pressure and mutual support.

1.5 In 1997 the Diocese of Guildford set up a working party to review the adequacy of stipends in the diocese. A survey of the clergy in the diocese was undertaken which revealed worrying levels of debt, widespread use of savings to make ends meet, reliance on gifts from a number of sources, anxiety about financial circumstances and the pressure on clergy families of unremitting vigilance about money. As a consequence, the Diocese announced in 1998 its decision to increase stipends by £1,500 over the following five years. This had the effect of putting Guildford well outside the amount of flexibility built into the national system.

1.6 Other dioceses regretted that Guildford had gone outside the national policy on stipends uniformity to such an extent. The then Chairman of the Consultative Group of Diocesan Chairmen and Secretaries, Mr Bryan Sandford, wrote to the Archbishop of York, Chairman of the House of Bishops' Standing Committee, to express the Group's deep concern about the unilateral breaking of the agreed national policy. The matter was discussed by the House of Bishops in October 1998.

1.7 Although there was concern about Guildford's action, there was agreement on the part of many people that the adequacy of the stipend did indeed need to be examined. Such an examination had been suggested by other dioceses (including Canterbury and Exeter) that had undertaken surveys among clergy, and by the Clergy and Churchworkers section of the Manufacturing Science and Finance Union (MSF), which had called for all incumbents to be paid at the level of residentiary canons.

1.8 In the preface to the 1999 edition of the *Church of England Year Book*, Canon Hugh Wilcox, Prolocutor of the Lower House of the Convocation of Canterbury and a member of the Archbishops' Council, also raised the question of the adequacy of the stipend. He called for an in-depth review. The Church was, he said, 'being subsidised in practice by working spouses'. In addition, ministers who 'are entirely reliant on the stipend find it very difficult to cope, especially if they have ageing relatives or dependent children'. Canon Wilcox suggested that the current position was contrary to Scripture and called upon the Archbishops' Council to give a lead.

1.9 In March 1999 the Finance Committee and the Deployment, Remuneration and Conditions of Service Committee of the Archbishops' Council, by now the Central Stipends Authority, both agreed to recommend to the Council that a working party should be set up to conduct a wide-ranging review of clergy stipends. The Council agreed to this recommendation at its meeting in April 1999.

1.10 The membership of the Review Group, which was appointed by the Council, together with the terms of reference for the work are set out at the front of this report.

the Review Group's methodology

1.11 The Group met 16 times between September 1999 and June 2001. The Group believed strongly that its deliberations had to take place within a theological context. Issues of vocation, scriptural principles, and the responsibility of the Christian community to its clergy were important throughout the discussions. Theological contributions were received from a number of people and are listed in the notes for Chapter 2.

1.12 The Group considered matters of principle with regard to the stipend, together with an assessment of its adequacy, prior to considering whether any proposed changes to the structure of clergy remuneration could be afforded, given the financial circumstances of the Church. The Group considered it essential to proceed in this way so that the Church could come to a mind in principle over the nature and the level of remuneration of its clergy.

1.13 The assessment of adequacy was addressed through:

- A survey of all stipendiary clergy and licensed lay workers on the central payroll;
- A consultation document sent to all General Synod members, the dioceses and other interested groups, advertised in the press and

available on request to any individual or group (The text of the consultation document is given at **Appendix 1**. The document elicited 344 responses.);

- Consultation with relevant clergy charities (A full list of those consulted is to be found in **Appendix 2**.);

- Consultation with the dioceses concerning charitable payments made to clergy from diocesan and other funds (A list of dioceses that responded is also to be found in **Appendix 2.**).

1.14 The survey was conducted by means of a questionnaire. Questionnaires were sent out to all stipendiary clergy and licensed lay workers on the central payroll. The survey was completely confidential and responses were received and processed by a research company, IRS (Information and Research Services). Non-stipendiary ordained spouses of clergy who were not reached by this mailing were able to request their own copy of the questionnaire. Clergy in the Diocese in Europe were invited to complete survey forms if they so wished.

1.15 Ten thousand questionnaires were sent out and 6,295 responses were received. Respondents included 100 licensed lay workers, 879 assistant clergy, 4,806 incumbents or clergy of incumbent status, 57 archdeacons, 13 deans or provosts, 18 bishops and 61 residentiary canons. The results were published in *Generosity and Sacrifice: The Results of the Clergy Survey* (CHP, 2001).

1.16 The information from all these sources provided significant evidence for the work of the Review Group in assessing whether the stipend does allow a member of the clergy to live without undue financial worry.

1.17 As part of its review, the Group began an assessment and consideration of the pension arrangements within the Church. In April 2001, the Church of England Pensions Board accepted the recommendations of its actuaries that the contribution rate for members of the pension scheme should rise in 2002 from 21.9% to 29.1% of the previous year's National Minimum Stipend for incumbents. The financial effect of this increase in the contribution rate (approximately £12m p.a.) will be significant for the dioceses.

1.18 In view of the effect that the increase in the contribution rate would have on the ability of the Church to fund any increase in stipends, the Group considered the impact on its own work. The Group believed that it had significant recommendations to make to the Church, whilst recognizing that the implementation of its recommendations could not be made in isolation from the financial position of the Church.

1.19   The Group was minded to suggest some changes to the pensions arrangements for clergy. However, following the outcome of the actuarial review, the Archbishops' Council set up a group on financial issues. As this group would itself be undertaking a consultation on future pension arrangements, the Review Group decided not to pursue work in this area. The areas to which the Group gave consideration are contained in Chapter 8, and we note that the Financial Issues Working Group will take these forward as part of its review.

the structure of the report

1.20   **Chapter 2** looks briefly at the history of the remuneration of the Church's ministers. It examines the scriptural principles and theological themes that should inform any discussion of the remuneration of the clergy. The chapter concludes by offering a new definition for the stipend.

1.21   Evidence relating to the financial circumstances of the clergy is described in some detail in **Chapter 3**. The evidence includes results from the survey, the responses to the consultation document, information gathered from charitable organizations set up to support clergy, and from dioceses. Comparisons are made between clergy remuneration and that of other professional groups and clergy of other churches.

1.22   One of the questions which absorbed a significant part of the Group's discussions was the value in the remuneration package to be placed on the provided house. The traditional approach has been to estimate the costs saved by a member of the clergy in not having to provide a house for him or herself. This has been done in the past by examining the costs that would be incurred by renting a semi-detached house. The chapter contains a recommendation about a new method of estimating the value. The chapter then asks whether the level of the stipend is reasonable and discusses a benchmark for the payment of stipends to which the Church might aspire.

1.23   The terms of reference for the work required the Review Group to look at the size of the differentials between stipends paid to clergy of incumbent status and those paid to bishops, deans and provosts, archdeacons and residentiary canons. These are discussed in **Chapter 4**. Comparisons are made with the remuneration structures in other professions and parts of the Church. Recommendations are made about simplifying the ratios between incumbents' stipends and those paid to dignitaries.

1.24   **Chapter 5** offers alternative structures for a new stipends system. The Group was committed to trying to maintain a high level of stipends coherence between dioceses. There was however division about the extent of the flexibility which might be given to dioceses before any notion of coherence was rendered meaningless. In the absence of agreement the Group offers the models described in Chapter 5 to the Church for extensive consultation in the hope that national agreement might be achieved on which model should be adopted.

1.25   Any change to the stipends system has implications for the work of the Central Stipends Authority. The future role envisaged for the CSA is described in **Chapter 6**.

1.26   **Chapter 7** examines the question of whether the 'tied house' should be retained and makes some recommendations about the future pattern of ownership of all clergy houses.

1.27   **Chapter 8** describes the present pension arrangements for clergy and licensed lay workers. It also raises some matters for discussion about the shape of future provision. The chapter makes a proposal that could, if developed, assist clergy in purchasing their own housing earlier in their ministry than the current retirement housing scheme allows.

1.28   Clergy expenses, taxation, job security and employment rights, and recommendations about additional earnings are discussed in **Chapter 9**. This also indicates some areas that the Review Group would like to be discussed with charitable bodies set up to assist clergy.

1.29   Finally, **Chapter 10** assesses the Group's recommendations in terms of their costs and affordability.

chapter 2

the remuneration of the clergy

setting the scene

2.1 The Group considered it an essential first principle of its work that the varied and complex matters under discussion should be informed by detailed theological reflection. This entailed significant engagement with Scripture and assessment of theological material received from a number of sources.[1]

2.2 The question of 'how the clergy should be paid' raises a wide range of issues, both theological and practical. The relationship of the clergy to wider society, the understanding of the kingdom of God, the nature of the ordained ministry, issues of service, sacrifice and reward all feature in the analysis. These matters are also influenced by historical considerations, differences in philosophy and by practical and pragmatic matters affecting the nature and level of remuneration, employment questions and financing arrangements; in other words, by clergy conditions of service.

2.3 We should not suppose that the current principles governing the definition of stipend are other than one particular approach adopted at a particular moment in the history of the Church. The current arrangements are, in fact, relatively recent.

2.4 Historically, the Church has adopted a wide variety of approaches to the remuneration of its ministers. Our knowledge of the precise arrangements for clergy remuneration in the early centuries of the Church is inevitably sketchy. However, as the Church grew in the third and fourth centuries so the matter of the support of the increasing number of clergy came to feature more particularly. By the end of the fifth century the Church in Rome had developed a system whereby all revenues were divided four ways, a quarter each going to support bishops, clergy, the poor and church repair.[2]

2.5 The relationship of Church and state has also affected clergy remuneration. In those areas where Christianity was adopted by the state in some form or other so endowments came to be made for the benefit of church and clergy. Certainly in England these included private endowments providing for the retention of a priest, perhaps to a family or an estate. All of this contributed to wide variations in clergy income and formed part of the catalyst for financial abuse and corruption surrounding the clerical office.

2.6 In 1836 the Ecclesiastical Commissioners began a process of reform, which included the first movements towards the equalization of clerical incomes by removing some endowments in the cases of the worst extremes; this process continued well into the twentieth century.

2.7 It was in this context that the House of Bishops in 1943 set out their definition of stipend:

> The stipends of the clergy have always, we imagine, been rightly regarded not as pay in the sense in which that word is understood in the world of industry today, not as reward for services rendered, so that the more valuable the service in somebody's judgement or the more hours worked, the more should be the pay, but rather as a maintenance allowance to enable the priest to live without undue financial worry, to do his work effectively in the sphere to which he is called and, if married, to maintain his wife and bring up his family in accordance with a standard which might be described as neither of poverty or riches ...

2.8 It is doubtful whether the stipends of the clergy of the Church of England have ever been paid in accordance with this definition. It holds within itself an inherent and unresolved tension between the view of the stipend as a maintenance allowance and the existence of differentials. The 1943 definition was itself affected by its own socio-economic setting as is the discussion today of clergy remuneration.

2.9 There are a number of factors which have developed over the last fifty years or so that point towards a new or refined definition of stipend. These factors include:

- Changing patterns of employment for spouses
- Expectations of clergy
- Perceived and actual examples of stipend inadequacy
- The role of the ordained priest in modern society
- Clergy couples
- Reform of other aspects of clergy conditions of service
- Deployment of clergy in the context of a reduced stipendiary workforce

- Theological debate and reflection upon the economic nature of society.

None of these factors should be implied as requiring a change in approach or definition in themselves; they do, however, point to the need for a thorough review which in itself should return us to scriptural and theological reflection.

2.10   In terms of the underlying philosophy that determines stipends, perhaps the crucial conceptual issue is whether the stipend should be understood as a maintenance allowance (in line with the 1943 definition) or whether the stipend should be understood more in the sense of salary, reward for the exercise of particular responsibilities. The Group would wish to reject the sharp dichotomy between these understandings that sees one as inherently more Christian than the other. There are examples of Christian organizations (e.g. Tearfund) where a professional pay structure is applied in a Christian environment without the negative implications of performance-related pay that some have associated with any salary-type approach to remuneration. More information about the Tearfund system is given in **Appendix 3**.

2.11   The Group is conscious of course that this report is the latest in a series of reports which have considered matters of stipend. The earlier reflections have usually been as part of wider subjects such as conditions of service or on particular matters such as differentials. We have made use of these reports in our own reflections though we differ from their conclusions in a number of ways. The reports which we have referred to include: *Differentials: A Report to the General Synod by the Central Stipends Authority*, 1977 (GS 333); *Clergy Conditions of Service: A Consultative Paper*, 1994 (GS 1126); *Improving Clergy Conditions of Service*, 1995 (GS 1173); a summary of responses and recommendations flowing from GS 1126, together with papers relating to the debate on the Diocese of Carlisle's motion on differentials debated in General Synod in 1996 and the *Report of Proceedings of the General Synod*.

2.12   Such reference was necessary to ensure that a full perspective was maintained of the development and debate within the Church over these matters over a significant period of time. It provides justification for a further and more comprehensive review of Scripture and theology in the light of both the changed context in which the Church finds itself, but more importantly, the need always to return to first principles, asking hard questions that are often avoided, not least in scriptural exegesis. It also acts as a warning to us not to baptize current practice with a status that does not properly take into account either those first principles or the historical development of the question – or at least not until those principles have been revisited afresh.

scriptural principles

2.13 In looking at the scriptural principles that should guide our discussion the Group has acknowledged a number of factors. Firstly, it is widely accepted that Scripture does not contain a blueprint for ministry, including matters of remuneration, that can simply be copied in the twenty-first century. Partly this is due to the lack of such detail in the Bible and partly due to the nature of modern society and changes in the way in which both society and Church are organized. Nevertheless, it is agreed that scriptural principles are foundational. Secondly, the overview of Scripture needs to be comprehensive, including reflection upon Old Testament provision for priests as well as New Testament passages. Thirdly, we need to recognize that commentators differ upon their interpretations of passages and there is a need to examine these differing interpretations. Fourthly, and perhaps most importantly, drawing upon the expertise available to the Group both within and beyond its formal membership, it was agreed that we should not be afraid to weigh the scriptural evidence afresh and draw appropriate conclusions to guide our work even if these differ to some degree from those of others before us.

the reward of priests and Levites in the Old Testament

2.14 A useful starting point was to look at the provision which was made in the Old Testament for the two groups of sanctuary servants, the priests and the Levites. The relationship between priest and Levite is not entirely clear from the Old Testament but it may help briefly to set out their development and purpose.

2.15 The priests were those descended from Aaron and his sons. In Exodus 28–29 Aaron and his sons, Nadab, Abihu, Eleazar and Ithamar were consecrated as priests. They alone were permitted to wear the priestly garments and carried specific responsibility for the offering of sacrifice at the altar, not least in the annual atonement ceremony (Exodus 30), which developed into the ritual of the Day of Atonement (Leviticus 16).

2.16 After the apostasy of the people of Israel with the Golden Calf (Exodus 32.25ff.) it was the Levites who rallied to Moses and avenged the disgrace that had been caused to the Lord's honour. This may account for the setting aside of the tribe of Levi for special service (Exodus 32.29). The Levites were designated as assistants to the priests and had particular responsibility for the dismantling, carrying and erecting of the tabernacle and also for its protection (Numbers 1.47-54). In 1 Chronicles 16 we see the Levites given the responsibility 'to make petition, to give thanks, and to praise the Lord ...'

2.17 In this analysis the concentration will be on the provision for the priests. Very similar provisions applied to the Levites and this is referred to where appropriate. Aaron and his descendants were one family from among the tribe of Levi; they were the priests, the rest of the tribe performed the ancillary functions of the Levites.

2.18 The priests were granted no part of the promised land of Canaan unlike all of the other tribes of Israel. This is clearly spelt out in Numbers 18.20:

> The Lord said to Aaron, 'You will have no inheritance in their land, nor will you have any share among them; I am your share and your inheritance among the Israelites.'

This at once introduces some notion of sacrifice, service and dependence upon God into the role of the priest but does not say anything about how the priest was to be provided for materially. This provision seems to have come from a number of sources, mainly:

- The first fruits
- Portions of sacrifices and offerings
- Tithe of the tithes.

the first fruits

2.19 As a thank-offering to God for the gift of the promised land, the people were to offer up to the Lord the choicest part of the crop (Exodus 23.19). This was represented in practice by the offering of grain, wine and oil. The first two of these were to be used in support of the priests (Numbers 18.12; Deuteronomy 18.4). The Book of Proverbs promises prosperity to those who honour the Lord with the first fruits (Proverbs 3.9). Not only were the Israelites to be mindful that the land of Canaan was the Lord's possession and that they had only the rights of tenants (Leviticus 25.23), but they were also to be aware that the fertility of Canaan's soil was not due to one of the Baals but rather to the Lord's gift of grace.

2.20   Theologically, it might be useful to make a connection from this to
the 'theology of gracious gift' which underpinned the 'Working As
One Body' process. Perhaps we might be helped to understand
the ministry/priesthood as God's gracious gift to us, which might
help towards a healthier view of the support of the Church's
ministers.

portions of sacrifices and offerings

2.21   Certain parts of animals used in sacrifice at the tabernacle were to be
reserved for the support of the priest. So, for example, in Exodus
29.27-34, the breast and thigh of the ram were to be 'the regular
share from the Israelites for Aaron and his sons. It is the contribution
the Israelites are to make to the Lord from their fellowship offerings.'
Similarly, for example, part of the grain offering (Leviticus 2.2,3), flour
from a sin offering (Leviticus 5.11-13) and the ram of the guilt
offering (Leviticus 7.6-10) were all to be reserved for the use of the
priests.

tithe of the tithes

2.22   The tithe, a tenth of the produce of the land, was primarily intended
for the support of the Levites (Numbers 18.24). The Levites were to
offer a tenth of this tithe (hence 'tithe of the tithes') as the Lord's
offering to support Aaron and the priests. It was described as
'an offering to the Lord' and was to represent 'the best and holiest
part of everything given to you' (Numbers 18.28,29). The rest of the
tithe received from the people of Israel was to be retained by the
Levites as, 'your wages for your work at the Tent of Meeting'
(Numbers 18.31).

2.23   There were other aspects to the support of priests including certain
redemption monies in the Jubilee (Leviticus 27.23) and part of the
spoils of war (Numbers 31.25-29). One further point is worth
mentioning. The priests and Levites did not receive a territorial
allotment in the settlement in Canaan but they were allocated towns
and cities to live in as stated in Leviticus 25.32-34; Numbers 35.2-8
and Joshua 21.1-4.

2.24   What kind of assessment can we make of these provisions? Two
principles might be said to emerge:

- The holiness of the priesthood, belonging essentially to God. Hence the role of the priest was to serve God in the sanctuary, and that which was reserved for the priest's use was to be the best or choicest parts.

- The priests were to be provided for out of the offerings of the people; this included provision in kind, in money and in property. The first call on the people's offerings were for the priest – this, of course, follows from the idea of the holiness of the priesthood.

We will need to consider subsequently how these principles are changed or not in the New Testament and how they might be applied to us today.

the reward of apostles, elders and overseers in the New Testament

2.25   The understanding of ministry in the New Testament Church is a developing theme. There are some general hints and pointers in the gospels which are somewhat further developed in the epistles as the appointment of elders/overseers in local churches became the established pattern. Nevertheless, there is not a fully worked-out understanding of church government or the provision of ministry as such in the New Testament.

principles from the gospels

2.26   The themes of sacrifice, service and yet also of appropriate reward, hinted at in the Old Testament material, retain a prominence in a number of places in the gospels, sometimes in juxtaposition to each other. In Luke 10:1-12 (parallels in Matthew 10 and Mark 6) Jesus sends out the 72 disciples to carry out the apostolic ministry of preaching and healing.

> Do not take a purse or bag or sandals; and do not greet anyone on the road. When you enter a house, first say, 'Peace to this house'. If a man of peace is there, your peace will rest on him; if not, it will return to you. Stay in that house, eating and drinking whatever they give you, for the worker deserves his wages.

What does this mean? On the face of it the 72 disciples are being exhorted to place their dependence upon God alone (i.e. 'take nothing with you'). Yet on the other, the reference to the worker deserving his wages, implies some obligation on the part of others to

13

provide for the disciples in their ministry. R.T. France, commenting on the Matthaean parallel, notes that this is not 'a call to asceticism', rather 'a call to put first things first'. He also refers to the reference to the worker being worth his keep as an important point for later Christian thought, referring to 1 Corinthians 9 and 1 Timothy 5.[3] Leon Morris in his commentary on Luke in the same series notes this:

> They are to have no compunction about receiving their meals free, for the labourer deserves his wages (cf. 1 Timothy 5.18). This is a principle of wide application that has sometimes been overlooked in Christian activities.[4]

Marshall notes that there is a certain tension here between the promise of material reward and the underlying warning against excess.[5] The reference to wages (*misthos*) means dues paid for work, reward resulting from labour.[6] The LXX[7] usage of *misthos* usually refers to the wage of a manual worker (Genesis 29.15; Exodus 2.9; Leviticus 19.13). There is criticism when payment is reduced (Deuteronomy 24.14), or withheld (Jeremiah 22.13) or beaten down (Malachi 3.5) or is paid late (Deuteronomy 24.15). This same word *misthos* is used in Numbers 18.31 for the payment of Levitical services in the sanctuary and also in Micah 3.11 for the remuneration of priests.

the evidence of the epistles

2.27   We will look separately at the two crucial passages of 1 Corinthians 9.1-23 and 1 Timothy 5.17,18. Firstly, however, we will review the other material.

other material from the epistles

2.28   The general point about self-sacrifice is reinforced in Acts 20:33,34, where Paul notes that 'these hands of mine have supplied my own needs and the needs of my companions'. This implies self-support and sacrifice. The point is reinforced in 1 Thessalonians 2.9 where Paul says that he worked night and day so as not to be a burden to them.

2.29   There is a very interesting short passage in 2 Corinthians. In chapter 11.7-9 Paul says this:

> Was it a sin for me to lower myself in order to elevate you by preaching the gospel of God to you free of charge? I robbed other churches by receiving support from them, so as to serve you. And when I was with you and needed something, I was not a burden to anyone, for the brothers who came from Macedonia supplied what I needed.

2.30 Clearly set out here is the principle of mutuality. Paul was supported in his gospel ministry by churches other than the one which he was immediately visiting. The interdependency of the gospel is shown by the fact that Paul accepted support from the Macedonian churches even though they knew extreme poverty (2 Corinthians 8.2). Yet he rejected support from the financially stronger Corinthian church. Alongside this remains that element of sacrifice and service that has appeared throughout; so in 2 Corinthians 12.15, Paul indicates: 'I will very gladly spend for you everything I have and expend myself as well.'

2.31 Similarly in Philippians 4.11, Paul refers to being content whatever the material circumstances. This is reinforced by Luke 3.14, which specifically refers to being content with pay. Certainly a warning against greed and avarice, but not licence to underpay Christian ministers! Failure to pay wages is a matter of justice (James 5.4).

1 Corinthians 9.1-23

2.32 This is an important and complicated passage that repays careful reading and study. Paul starts by asserting his apostolic rights: the right to food and drink (v.4), to family support (v.5) and even the general right to give up other work to work full-time for the gospel (v.6).

2.33 Paul then proceeds to draw comparisons with other employments. The soldier, owner of the vineyard and the shepherd all receive reward for their labours from their occupations. Indeed each of these employments is used elsewhere in Scripture as types for the Christian worker (2 Timothy 2.3-6; 1 Corinthians 3.6,7; John 21.15-17). Deuteronomy 25.4 is quoted; 'Do not muzzle an ox while it is treading out the grain.' The principle in the Law was that the ox was not to be muzzled so that it could partake of some of the grain it was threshing. Paul relates the Old Testament situation to the current circumstances. The principle is one of sharing in the harvest, materially as well as spiritually (vv.10-12). Indeed, 'the Lord has commanded that those who preach the gospel should receive their living from the gospel' (v.14). Paul was fully entitled to this material reaping. It was a right and indeed, a command.

2.34 The language used here of 'spiritual' and 'material' is the same as in Romans 15.27 where Paul speaks of the coming of the gospel to the Gentiles as 'spiritual blessings' and their collection for the poor in Jerusalem as 'material blessings'.[8] So also with his work for the gospel in Corinth. The reference to the Lord's command that those who preach the gospel should receive their living from the gospel is, in Fee's view, a reference to Luke 10.7, which we have already discussed.[9]

2.35 However, the double strand that seems to have run throughout this analysis of the right to material provision on the one hand and sacrifice and service on the other also appears here. Paul, after setting out in some detail the rights he could claim to material support, then proceeds to emphasize that he has surrendered these rights (1 Corinthians 9 v.15). However, we should at once note, with Morris, that the fact that Paul did not exercise this right to be maintained by the church itself implies that others did so, indeed other apostles.[10] He also makes the point, in verses 4-6, that it is the general right to maintenance that Paul is referring to and that his surrender of that right is not 'a confession of ineligibility'.[11]

2.36 Paul sets out his overriding purpose, to preach the gospel. For Paul, nothing, not even his own rights to material support, must get in the way of preaching the good news of the gospel. If he carried out the task voluntarily he would indeed merit a reward; in fact he is compelled to do so, simply discharging the trust that has been placed in him. *Misthos* (reward) carries no understanding of grace; it is payment for work done.[12] His reward is simply that of preaching the gospel of free grace (verses 17,18).

2.37 Gordon Fee offers evidence that Paul had moved from patronage and support provided by congregations (as evidenced in Acts 16.15) to self-support with his tent-making, perhaps in order to more particularly distinguish himself from current philosophical peddlers.[13]

2.38 Fee goes on to comment on verses 1-14:

> The whole reason for the argument is to assert that his giving up of these rights does not mean that he is not entitled to them ... On the other hand, the reason he feels compelled to make this kind of defence is that he has given up these rights. Contemporary ministers seldom feel compelled so to argue! ... All too often, one fears, the objective of this text is lost in concerns over 'rights' that reflect bald professionalism rather than a concern for the gospel itself.[14]

And later:

> Those who see their calling as 'necessity laid upon them' should also be glad to readjust their lives for the sake of the gospel.[15]

1 Timothy 5.17-18

2.39 'The elders who direct the affairs of the church well are worthy of double honour, especially those whose work is preaching and teaching. For the Scripture says, "Do not muzzle the ox while it is treading out the grain" and "The worker deserves his wages".' [16]

2.40 The reference is to 'elders'. The Greek is *presbyteroi*. The word is plural and also appears elsewhere in the pastoral epistles, including Titus 1.5 where Paul refers to the appointment of church leaders. It is from this word that we derive presbyter or priest in the ordinal. The prime reference is to a local church leader. These elders are those who have been appointed to the leadership of the local church to rule, lead or direct. [17] The word for 'rule', *proistemi*, is used by Paul for those who exercise leadership in the local congregation (1 Thessalonians 5.12; Romans 12.8). Following Justin Martyr and other commentators this general leadership may also be seen as including presidency of the Eucharist.

2.41 The word for 'honour' – *time* – has already been used in this chapter in verse 3 in reference to widows. In that instance there is a clear reference to material provision as well as reverence and respect. Thus it is quite reasonable to conclude that the same double usage is appropriate here. The elders involved in the direction of the church are worthy of double honour – that is, two-fold respect and two-fold remuneration. This understanding is certainly supported by at least one leading Greek Lexicon, specifically quoting 1 Timothy 5.17,18 as likely to be carrying this double meaning. [18] The word is used in the sense of 'pay' in Matthew 27.6,9; Acts 4.34; 7.16 and 1 Corinthians 6.20. Calvin also understood the reference to mean double recompense. [19] The combination of the context and the link with Deuteronomy 25.4 and Luke 10.7 suggests strongly that a monetary reward is in view, especially for those who labour in preaching and teaching, which are matters of great importance in the pastoral epistles. This view is widely supported by biblical commentators. [20]

2.42 Which elders are in view? It may be a reference to all elders, or, more likely given the context, it may be a sub-group with particular responsibilities for preaching and teaching, as opposed to overseers in general, all of whom must be able to teach (1 Timothy 3.2). Some exegetes draw a distinction between the use of *episcopos* – singular, as a reference to bishop – and, *presbyteroi* – plural, as a reference to elders/presbyters to justify the episcopate as this sub-group, but it is more likely that this is a reference to a wider sub-group; the distinction between bishop and elder in the pastoral epistles is actually much less clear, if it exists at all. The wider ministry of the bishop is represented in Scripture more by Paul's commissioning of Timothy and Titus.

2.43 In verse 18 there is appeal to two scriptural quotations in support. The first quote is from Deuteronomy 25.4, which is also quoted in our other major passage of 1 Corinthians 9. We have already seen how in that passage Paul relates this quotation to the reaping of material, not just spiritual, reward. It is also apparent that the two quotations used by Paul here are intended to be linked; the second quote, 'the worker deserves his wages' unambiguously refers to material reward, so also we should assume does the former.

2.44 The other quote comes from Luke 10.7 (paralleled in Matthew 10.10). G.W. Knight maintains that this reference to 'wages' refers to payment for work done and that Jesus is stating the justness of wages on this basis.[21] He is, in principle, here following the accepted definition of *misthos*. See also the comments on 1 Corinthians 9.

2.45 To quote Donald Guthrie:

> ... he intends Timothy to understand that a divine sanction underlies the principle of fair provision for those who serve the church. Too often a niggardly attitude has been maintained towards faithful men who have laboured for Christ in the interests of others.

> The apostle has already deplored money-grabbing (3.3), but equally he deplores inadequate remuneration. If God ordained ample provision for oxen treading out corn, it is incumbent upon Christian communities to see that those who devote time and energy to their service are adequately rewarded.'[22]

2.46 Certainly among early church documents the Apostolic Constitutions reflect this understanding:

> As much as is given to each one of the elder women, let double that amount be given to the deacons, in honour of Christ. Let also a double portion be set apart for the presbyters ... If there is a reader, let him receive a single portion.
>
> Apostolic Constitutions 7.411

2.47 More generally referring to Luke 10.7 the bishop is bidden to:

> view such food and clothing sufficiently as meets necessity and decency. Let him not make use of the Lord's goods as another's. Rather, let him

> use them moderately, 'for a labourer is worthy of his reward.' Let him be
> not luxurious in diet or fond of idle furniture ... Let him use as a man of
> God those tithes and first-fruits that are given according to the command
> of God.
>
> Apostolic Constitutions 7.408

2.48 On insight into how the clergy were materially supported in the early
church:

> Those who attend upon the church should be maintained by the church –
> as being priests, Levites, presidents, and ministers of God.
>
> Apostolic Constitutions 7.409

conclusions from the biblical material

2.49 What conclusions might we be able to draw from this review of the
biblical material, plus some patristic material? It has to be said again
that the Bible does not contain a fully worked-out system for the
remuneration of the stipendiary clergy of the Church of England at the
start of the third Christian millennium. Nevertheless, the Bible
remains the basic building block of the Church and the pointers and
principles in the Bible are of foundational importance for our guidance
in this matter as much as in any other. Let us offer some tentative
observations and conclusions:

- The exercise of biblical exposition and review is possible and
  essential to the process.

- Throughout the Old Testament and the New Testament there are
  parallel strands on the right to material provision for those in
  ministry and the sacrificial nature of the priesthood/ministry. This is
  expressed in a number of ways, not least in terms of contentment,
  sacrifice of rights and self-support.

- There is no evidence of material provision being at or near
  subsistence levels, though there are warnings against opulence
  and luxury. The 1943 definition can be seen as encouraging
  such an approach though we accept that it was not intended
  to do so.

- In principle the responsibility for providing for the ministry lies with
  the offerings of the people.

- There is clear evidence of mutuality, the rich supporting the poor,
  and also of sacrificial giving by the poor.

- It is clear that those specially entrusted with preaching and teaching are deemed in the New Testament to be entitled to higher remuneration. The question is whether this applied to all elders or only some. There may be some justification in seeing this group as most closely represented by the stipendiary clergy. In any event this moves us further away from a 'living allowance stipend' and at least opens up for us the discussion of differentials.

- The 'wages' referred to in the New Testament clearly refer to payment for work done.

- The provision for priests in the Old Testament was to be of the best, choicest elements of the first fruits and tithes. It represented the first call upon the offerings of the people.

- Two leading commentators, Gordon Fee and Donald Guthrie, comment rather differently on the implications of all this. Guthrie suggests that Christian communities have failed to ensure adequate provision for workers, while Fee suggests that the notion of sacrifice has been lost amid the battle for 'rights'.

- Perhaps one principle we could work with would be 'generous and just' alongside the idea of 'service and sacrifice.'

- We could also make some use of the 'theology of gracious gift' as investing the ministry with a God-given value, emphasizing the ministry as God's gracious gift to us. That might encourage a greater understanding and commitment to the provision and financing of the ministry.

theological models

2.50   The Group requested and received a number of submissions dealing with the application of theological principles and models to the question of remuneration for the clergy. A number of key theological themes underpinned much of the evidence and discussion.

the nature of ordained ministry

2.51   The nature of the call to ordained ministry is distinctive and particular. It arises out of a call from God to the minister which, although affirmed by the Church, remains in essence a call from God. The Church has quite rightly from the time of the Reformation recovered the concept of vocation and calling in a much broader context than ordained ministry – though, of course, historically, vocation has always been a very strong element in callings to the religious life. However, the distinctiveness of ordained ministry is that this call is to a ministry of word and sacrament in a particular context. This may be in the context of a local congregation (presbyter/deacon) or more widely (prophet/ apostle) – the latter demonstrated within some sort of institutional setting by Timothy and Titus. Thus in the nature and exercise of this call the nature of ordained ministry is different from any other employment. Indeed, this call is an intrinsic feature of the minister's life.

2.52 There is, however, something of a tension between this distinctiveness of the ordained minister – which might indeed lead us away from following secular employment models and practices – and the realities of the professional clergy person in the twenty-first century. What is distinctive is the conferring of ministerial orders. For most clergy, however, the practice of ministry reflects much more secular patterns of employment; for some very closely so. Thus, a stipend is attached to a post, which can only be exercised through a bishop's licence (though the minister is viewed as integrally sharing the ministry of the bishop). Clergy are increasingly expected to follow guidelines regarding professional conduct, continuing ministerial education and basic duties and, *in extremis*, a minister can be removed from his or her post by due process. For a few clergy, primarily those in chaplaincies and sector ministries, this process may include contracts of employment, professional assessment and in some cases a scale of salaried payments. The professional minister in the twenty-first century operates within a framework of canonical, legal and moral constraints upon the individual's ministry. It is perhaps this tension in practice that has led to increasing recognition of the inadequacies of the present arrangements and the need for reform, not just, of course, in the matter of stipends.

eschatology and the Kingdom of God – the concept of the interim

2.53 The importance of eschatology in the Christian understanding of the world and, indeed, in the nature of the relationship to the world has been long appreciated. In essence the incarnation of Jesus marked the inauguration of the kingdom of God on earth, and yet until the Lord's return and the consummation of all things that kingdom is not revealed in all its fullness. In short we live in the interim. Much disagreement among Christians with regard to the nature of our engagement with the world stems from variations in our understanding of the relationship of this world and the next.

2.54   Thus, in our engagement with society the Christian Church cannot ignore, for example, the impact of economic competition upon us. The question is how, and to what extent, should the Christian embrace or stand over and against such concepts. Christians will vary in their approach and this can sometimes be uncomfortable. Thus those of more liberal approach will reflect upon the world around us and ask what insights from the world can inform us of the nature of God's kingdom. The more conservative will tend to reflect upon the world from the standpoint of Scripture and tradition and ask what insights these authorities shed upon the world in which we live. The crucial issues we face though are as a result of the interaction of the kingdom of God and the created world and will be affected by where we stand on the continuum of Christian belief. Hence we need to reflect very carefully upon secular models so that we are informed by important insights but also so that our Christian beliefs determine the nature of the extent to which we embrace such concepts.

2.55   The economic concept of scarcity – including scarcity and price of labour resources – is a consequence of living in the interim. Indeed, work and remuneration have been factors in the world in which we have been placed by God ever since the creation – work does not just derive from the fall. Recruitment, reward and retention are all factors related to economic value and scarcity, and they affect the Church as much as any other institution. Taken to its logical economic conclusion, the effect of this is that the rate of pay of salaried clergy would fluctuate in order to secure sufficient clergy of the right calibre, and might rise in accordance with responsibilities (number of parishes, wider church responsibilities).

2.56   However, the interaction between the distinctive, divine calling of a minister of word and sacrament and the economic realities of the period of the interim act as constraints upon each other. Hence, it may well be that the Church cannot avoid the economic forces affecting its own labour market, yet the distinctiveness of the Christian calling to ordained ministry will act as a constraint upon them. Hence, on the supply side, the economic curve relating the numbers of clergy available to be employed to their remuneration (i.e. the economic relationship between quantity and price of labour) may be shallower than for other professions. In other words clergy are prepared to supply their services for less, hence offering more pay will only slightly increase the numbers of clergy. Similarly, on the demand side, the Church may be less willing to pay salaries related to the local market since it wishes to maintain its theological concept of a national church which requires a degree of clergy mobility.

2.57   It is the interaction of these factors that determines the current situation regarding clergy remuneration. The extent of dissatisfaction with these arrangements, of which there is some evidence, is a sign that the arrangements have fallen out of equilibrium even when taking into account the constraints on economics forces discussed above.

remuneration models

2.58   There are a number of different approaches that could be taken to these relationships. The document *Clergy Conditions of Service: A Consultative Paper*, 1994 (GS 1126) referred to some possible alternatives to the traditional stipend, namely market forces, individual performance, value to the organization and length of service. We would wish to reflect on three theological models which encompass a range of alternative approaches including those listed above.

2.59   The **counter-cultural model** is the one that reflects most closely a fully-worked out application of the stipend as a maintenance allowance principle. It emphasizes that the Church is not a business or a secular organization. It places the greatest weight upon the distinctiveness of the call to gospel ministry over and against the cultural influences of the world. Hence there will be greater equality between ministers, differentials would be removed and indeed families would be expected to share the economic hardships of the clergy life. There are many in the Church who find this model compelling as a Christian lifestyle.

2.60   The implications of this model should not be either overstated or romanticized. There may be a superficial attraction to some to remove the differentials of the relatively small number of ordained ministers who hold office as bishops, archdeacons or other posts of responsibility. The model could however provide for differentials on the basis of need which would lead to clergy of widely differing circumstances and responsibilities receiving significantly different stipends. However, the implications of this approach are also that the cleric could have little claim to stipend increases above the Retail Prices Index (i.e. price inflation). Any claim or suggestion that there should be any form of benchmarking or comparison with other professions or any claim to comparability even to the Average Earnings Index (i.e. wage inflation) would be nonsense with this model. The key features are sacrifice and subsistence. The consequence would be an ever-increasing gap between the majority of clergy and the majority of others.

2.61   The **contractual model**. This approach recognizes that the Church is not immune from the increasingly individual and market-orientated world in which we live and effectively seeks an accommodation with the world while not necessarily embracing every aspect of the contract culture. Clergy would be employees with legally binding contracts. Freehold of office would disappear and there would be increasing paraphernalia of management; standards and assessment of performance, accountability and discipline, compensated for by a clear salary structure. Differentials between clergy would most likely widen.

2.62   Again the implications of this must not be avoided. Although it would not inevitably do so, such a model could shift the Church towards a system of performance-related pay. This would carry significant implications for the assessment and grading between clergy who, on the face of it, were experiencing the same call to the same ministry. There would be considerable loss of local autonomy and freedom to the clergy and although employment practices, in terms of human resources management, might improve, this would be accompanied by cases before industrial tribunals and secular courts.

2.63   The **status quo**, the current model, is a compromise largely based upon the counter-cultural approach but influenced also in a number of areas by the more secular contractual model. This model carries with it a number of inherent tensions, which have contributed to the pressure for reform. Thus, differentials are maintained within a model which claims to be a maintenance allowance. The process by which stipends are set includes comparisons with other professional groups and both price inflation and average earnings.

2.64   The Group believes that there is a fourth way, which might perhaps be described as the sacrificial model. Sacrificial because it requires sacrifice on the part of the clergy (who, therefore, would not be claiming the right to be remunerated as other, perhaps comparable, professional groups) and sacrifice also on the part of the whole church (recognizing the need for a properly remunerated professional ministry). This approach places great emphasis upon the need for professional models of remuneration for Christian ministry and accepts the need for some recognition of responsibility and for generosity in the setting of the level of pay. It recognizes however that both clergy and laity are called to sacrifice and generosity. It does seek to place these emphases within a more coherent framework, firmly based upon Scripture and with a theological foundation which is more widely understood. How this might be worked out in practice is discussed in the next section.

2.65 The theological models set out above may sometimes seem to establish too strong a dichotomy between the understanding of salary and its implications and the traditional view of stipend. The Group believes that clear thinking is essential to the process of reviewing stipends. We must neither invest a traditional understanding with undue weight that it might not be able to bear nor characterize any approach with implications that are not necessarily warranted.

2.66 The idea of a maintenance allowance is not entirely alien to a salary-based system. All systems of reward or remuneration include within them considerations of adequacy based partly on human need and dignity. Such concerns are not the sole preserve of a maintenance allowance system. Indeed, if the consequence of a maintenance allowance approach has been to result in inadequate stipends then any possible claim for such a system to be morally superior begins to be challenged. In addition many of the responsibilities of clergy are the same as those skills required in much of secular employment, including leadership, vision, caring and vocation.

2.67 Questions of value, morale, recruitment and retention are all relevant questions to take into account in the setting of stipends even in the context of Christian ministry, even if they are not to be the determining factors. A workforce with low morale and poor pay will be a disincentive to recruitment and retention even if financial reward is not the principal determining factor in such vocations.

2.68 All of this opens up further questions on which the Church may need to engage in continued debate. These issues include whether the Church desires in the longer-term to have a smaller number of better-paid clergy, with perhaps greater accountability and stricter selection criteria, given what will be the increasing demands of the work and responsibilities involved.

2.69 The Group believes in the development of a model consistent with biblical and theological principles and that it is possible to ensure a professional pay structure for clergy that gives recognition to both need and responsibility and to the particular training and qualifications of the clergy, while recognizing that the distinctive nature of the calling is such that clergy would neither expect nor receive the same level of remuneration as comparable professionals in commerce.

2.70 It might be helpful at this point to comment on the question of performance-related pay. This approach gained little support from either the survey of clergy or the consultation process. It also did not gain support from within the Review Group. It is undoubtedly true that performance-related pay might in itself have generated an aura of suspicion within many groups (not least the public sector) that is unwarranted. This sort of approach to reward is not uncommon in the private sector. The Group, however, believes that there is a case for some degree of reward for the extent of responsibility undertaken and that this might indeed have implications for job descriptions, appointment procedures and job evaluation, but that it would be divisive and contrary to our understanding of the distinctiveness of ordained ministry to explicitly link pay to performance targets.

2.71 The survey and consultation exercise undertaken revealed a wide variety of comment upon the nature of stipends and future direction. Almost all of the various alternative understandings were advocated by some. The majority preferred an approach closer to the counter-cultural model set out above that would imply the removal of stipend differentials and possibly the use of child allowances. There were, nevertheless, some significant submissions that addressed creatively the matters with which the Group is concerned. These submissions included comment from individual clergy, lay people, Diocesan Boards of Finance and clergy charities. Nevertheless, all of these groups also reflected the broad range of opinion. For the reasons discussed above and summarized in our conclusions below the Review Group believe that it is both right and appropriate to recommend some adjustments in our understanding and application of the notion of stipend.

the Group's new definition of stipend

2.72 The Group believes that this detailed review of scriptural and theological principles is foundational to any proper assessment of the nature and methodology of clergy remuneration and must form the basis of any proposals for amendment.

2.73 It is clear to the Group that the current position, purportedly based upon the 1943 House of Bishops' definition of a stipend, is flawed. Actual practice does not reflect that definition now, even if it ever did. The definition provides no basis for the existence of differentials, including some that already exist between parochial clergy. It fails to hold together competing tensions within it and seems to have been, at least in part, a formula that has resulted in unacceptably low levels of remuneration for the clergy. It fails to ask proper questions of how a professional system of remuneration within a Christian framework might operate. Upon closer investigation its basis in Scripture and theology is questionable.

2.74 There is, we are aware, a considerable body of opinion within the Church, reflected to some degree in our survey of clergy, that holds strongly to an approach to clergy stipends that closely reflects the counter-cultural model we have described. Opinion nevertheless remains divided and it is our responsibility to reflect upon this, weigh the evidence before us and make any necessary recommendations.

2.75 It is also clear to us that if the Church were to adopt the counter-cultural approach it would need to do so in its entirety if it were to maintain any form of integrity to its Christian witness. It is simply incompatible with this approach to expect clergy to be remunerated on the basis of a maintenance allowance and pay differentials to holders of posts of responsibility.

2.76 The Group, however, finds this position, however laudable and appealing it may at first sight seem, to be found wanting in Scripture. We could find no scriptural evidence that supported a system of paying a maintenance or subsistence allowance to ministers. Indeed, our conclusion from the scriptural evidence was rather to the contrary.

2.77 Nevertheless, it is also the case that as a Group we find the embracing of a full contractual system of employment relations, with all the implications for assessments of value to an organization and possibly performance-related pay, also to be inappropriate to the nature of the ministerial office and to be unsupported in Scripture where there was considerable emphasis upon sacrifice, calling and service.

2.78 The dilemma then is how to resolve these tensions within a model that does not collapse under the weight of inconsistency. We wish to affirm an approach that reflects the demands of Scripture and also takes serious account of theological reflection upon the relationship between the Church and the world. It is clear to us from consideration of the methods of reward and remuneration used in other Christian organizations such as Tearfund and other mission agencies that it is possible to construct some form of professional remuneration system for the Christian clergy that is consistent with the principles of Scripture and which recognizes the reality of pay as compensation or reward for professional services but which does not imply the full acceptance of the secular world of contract.[23]

2.79 **The Group recommends, for the reasons stated above, the retention of the concept of stipend, but modified in understanding and definition.**

2.80 We believe that it is possible to work with the key principles from the scriptural analysis of generosity and sacrifice and produce a succinct definition of stipend for the guidance of the Church and then to associate with that definition a longer list of principles to guide its application.

2.81 **The Group's definition of stipend is:**

> **The stipend is part of the remuneration package which is paid for the exercise of office. It reflects the level of responsibility held. This package acknowledges the dual demands in Scripture of generosity and sacrifice on both those who receive the stipend and those who raise the necessary funds.**

2.82 **Two guidelines for application should be adopted.** Firstly, that the principle adopted is that of 'remuneration for the exercise of office' rather than a 'maintenance allowance'. This has a number of implications.

- The principle of differentials for responsibility is allowed for.
- Subsistence levels of pay are not allowed for.
- Pay should be related to posts, not households or personal circumstances.
- Circumstantial maintenance payments (e.g. child allowances) are not allowed for.

2.83 The second guiding principle is that of 'generosity and sacrifice'. This would suggest the following implications:

- Clergy remuneration should represent a primary call on the budgets of the Church, national, diocesan and parochial.
- The reasonable expectation of the clergy that any comparisons made are with professional secular groups does not in itself imply that comparable remuneration should be paid.
- Benefits in kind are properly taken into account in determining remuneration.
- Differentials, where paid, should be modest.

2.84 It must be stated explicitly that this definition is a significant change in the basic methodology underlying our approach as a Church to stipend. It inculcates a move in principle away from 'a maintenance allowance' to 'reward for the exercise of office'. We believe that this is a more honest approach, allows us to achieve greater coherence and is consistent with scriptural teaching. We have not, however, sought to embrace a full contractual approach to the matter of stipends. Hence we believe that differentials are permitted in principle but should be restricted in size. We believe that this approach allows for a greater balance of justice and need in stipends and allows for the usual understanding of stipend adequacy to be replaced by a greater emphasis not just on reasonableness but on generosity. All of this, of course, will operate within the scriptural framework of sacrifice and service which rightly reflects our shared understanding of the nature of ordained ministry.

2.85 **We recommend that the definition of stipend set out in paragraph 2.81 be adopted along with the principles of application detailed in paragraphs 2.82 and 2.83.**

chapter 3
the level of the stipend

current stipend levels

3.1   The stipends of parochial clergy and licensed lay workers are set by the dioceses in the light of recommendations from the Archbishops' Council in its role as Central Stipends Authority (CSA). Details of the current stipends system, levels of stipend and other components of the remuneration 'package' are shown in **Appendix 4**.

3.2   The main recommendations made by the CSA are a National Minimum Stipend for incumbents (£16,040 in 2001) and a National Stipend Benchmark (£16,910 in 2001). The National Minimum Stipend (NMS) is the level below which no full-time incumbent or clergyperson of incumbent status should be paid unless there are exceptional circumstances. The National Stipend Benchmark (NSB) indicates to dioceses the level of stipend that the CSA recommends to be paid to incumbents.

3.3   The CSA also sets Regional Stipend Benchmarks for each diocese, which adjust the level of the NSB, so that stipends provide approximately the same purchasing power for all areas of the country when the effect of regional variations in the cost of living are taken into account. This enables dioceses in the more expensive areas of the country to pay higher stipends. Dioceses are asked to set their stipends neither more than 2.5% above nor less than 1.5% below their Regional Stipend Benchmark. In 2001/02, two dioceses paid above the 2.5% limit and two dioceses paid below the 1.5% limit.

3.4   In 2001/02, the national average stipend for incumbents was £17,030 – £120 more than the CSA's National Stipend Benchmark of £16,910. In general terms, amounts paid to clergy of incumbent status ranged from the National Minimum Stipend of £16,040 to the residentiary canons' figure of £20,800.

3.5   On the whole, the majority of parochial incumbent status clergy receive the same stipend in a diocese. The residentiary canons' figure is used in some dioceses for sector ministry posts, and for diocesan posts such as Directors of Education or Youth Officers.

However generalizations are difficult, as the level of remuneration for such posts varies from diocese to diocese, as does the nature of the responsibilities involved; these clergy may be paid a salary or a stipend and perhaps a housing allowance, while sometimes, they receive the same stipend as incumbents in that diocese.

increases in the level of stipend

3.6 In recent years, the trend has been for increases in the CSA's recommendations to increase by more than the increase in the Retail Price Index (RPI) but by less than the Average Earnings Index (AEI). If the stipend is regarded purely as a living allowance, then it can be argued that, if the stipend is at an adequate level, there is no need for stipends to increase by more than RPI. However, the new definition of stipend as payment for the exercise of office suggests that increases should exceed RPI.

3.7 This does not necessarily mean, however, that increases should be linked to AEI, which is arguably distorted by a few unusually high earners, not typical of the majority of employees. AEI cannot be used as a direct point of comparison with the incomes of parishioners as it does not include incomes from pensions and social security benefits in its calculation. Nevertheless, AEI retains some value as a general indicator of what is happening to earnings nationally, and this value is enhanced if the new stipend definition is adopted.

approaches adopted by the Group

3.8 The Group adopted various approaches, when considering the level of the stipend. These are discussed in further detail below and included:

- Commissioning a survey of all clergy and licensed lay workers on the central payroll;
- Issuing a consultation document for discussion throughout the Church;
- Comparing the Church of England's stipend provision with that of other churches;
- Re-examining the value of the clergy remuneration package and comparing clergy income with other professions.

consultations carried out by the Group

3.9   In order to obtain a broad spectrum of opinion on the level of the stipend, the Group initiated two consultation processes. First it commissioned an independent market research company, Information & Research Services (IRS), to conduct a survey among all stipendiary clergy and licensed lay workers on the central payroll. This survey was supported financially by a grant from the Ecclesiastical Insurance Group. The second approach was to issue a consultation document for discussion throughout the Church by clergy, lay people, PCCs and other interested groups.

(a) the survey of stipendiary clergy and licensed lay workers

3.10   Summary results of the survey were as follows:

- 5,448 men and 807 women responded. (40 did not state their gender.) The respondents included 5,100 married and 1,077 single people.
- 6,078 respondents (96%) lived in provided housing.
- Nearly three-fifths (57%) of married clergy had spouses who worked outside the home.
- Over one-third (35%) of these earned annual incomes of below £5,000, one quarter (25%) between £5,000–£10,000, one quarter (28%) between £10,000–£20,000, and one-sixth (15%) over £20,000.
- Over 4,000 grants or gifts were made to clergy from charities, diocesan funds, families and friends, and parishioners during 1999/2000 (excluding any made towards debt relief). Multiple responses were possible to this question, as some respondents may have received grants or gifts from more than one source.
- Over two-thirds (68%) of respondents stated that they had no debts.
- Of those with debt, two-fifths (41%) said that their debts had increased during the last year.
- 225 grants or gifts had been made to help pay off debts during the last year, though multiple responses were possible to this question.
- One-twentieth (5%) of all respondents had received or said that they would claim Working Families Tax Credit.
- For those clergy where the stipend was the sole source of income, one-third (33%) either struggled to pay their bills or else struggled to provide extra things such as holidays.

- Nearly two-fifths (38%) of respondents with capital reserves had had to draw on these during the previous year to meet their normal living costs. This proportion rose to over three-fifths (61%) for households with dependent children where there was no or little additional income.

- Over half (56%) of respondents said that their parishes could not afford to pay a higher stipend. Over a quarter (28%) said that their parishes could contribute more. One-sixth (16%) did not answer this question.

- Nearly one-third (32%) of respondents chose not to answer the question of what would be a reasonable stipend. Of the options given, between £19,000 and £21,000 p.a. was the most popular choice, and this was favoured by over a quarter (28%) of respondents. Another quarter (23%) of respondents expressed contentment with a stipend below £19,000, as compared with just under one-fifth (17%) of respondents, who supported options above £21,000 p.a.

- Nearly two-thirds (65%) of respondents either agreed or strongly agreed that child allowances should be paid. Of these over three-quarters (78%) either agreed or strongly agreed that they should be means tested against household income. One-fifth (21%) of respondents disagreed or strongly disagreed with the principle of child allowances.

- Of those receiving just the stipend nearly half (49%) stated that their standard of living was equivalent to or above the standard of living of the majority of households in their parish compared with slightly fewer (47%) who stated that it was below. Of clergy in households where there was income in addition to the stipend, two-thirds (67%) stated that their standard of living was equivalent to or above the standard of living of the majority of households in their parish compared with three-tenths (29%) who stated that it was below.

- Over nine-tenths (92%) of clergy rated their job satisfaction as adequate or above (with three-quarters (74%) as good or excellent).

3.11 Care needs to be taken when considering these results in isolation, as they may reveal an expectation – that is shared across all walks of life – that remuneration is less than it should be. However, the professional advice of those who analysed the results for us was that the job satisfaction figures for clergy were substantially higher than for the population at large. This is borne out by a recent survey quoted in the *Guardian* which indicated that four out of ten British workers declared themselves 'very satisfied' with their jobs. A second survey, undertaken for *The New Statesman* (July 2000), indicated that, across the working population, nearly three-fifths (57%) of people considered that they enjoyed their jobs.

clergy with dependent children

3.12 A further analysis was carried out to see to what extent clergy with dependent children, particularly those with a non-earning or low-earning spouse, or no spouse at all, were worse off than other clergy. The results of this exercise were as follows:

	Percentage of all respondents	Percentage of clergy with dependent children and non-earning or low-earning spouse	Percentage of clergy with dependent children and no spouse
Receiving or have received Working Families Tax Credit	5	11	10
In receipt of state benefits other than child benefit	4	9	10
Debts of less than £2,000	13	15	17
£2,000–£4,000	9	8	11
£5,000–£10,000	4	3	7
more than £10,000	3	3	6
Have some savings	77	75	61
Have added to savings	38	22	20
Have not added to savings	55	72	74
Make regular savings	68	64	53
Drew on savings	29	45	37
Own residential property	38	32	25

3.13 It is clear that assistant staff are likely to be over represented in the group of clergy that are hard-pressed financially. Given that all but a few incumbents are paid well above the National Minimum Stipend for incumbents, **we recommend that the current National Minimum Stipend should apply to all clergy, and not only incumbents as at present**.

3.14 **We also recommend that there should be a corresponding increase in the stipend for incumbents. At present the National Stipend Benchmark is 1.05 of the National Minimum Stipend. We recommend that it should be increased to 1.1 of the National Minimum Stipend.** This is further explored in Chapter 5.

additional payments

3.15 As well as additional payments for additional responsibility, additional payments to parochial clergy for a variety of other reasons used to be fairly common. The main payments were as follows:

>Allowances for long service
Contributions towards expenses
Child allowances
Provision to retain a certain portion of fee income
Area-based additional payments
Large number of parishes allowance.

3.16 The practice of making additional payments for length of service has largely died out. In its booklet *The Parochial Expenses of the Clergy: A Guide to their Reimbursement*, the CSA recommends that parishes should not make block allowances for expenses, as a 1989 survey indicated that clergy are less likely to receive full reimbursement of their expenses if this method is used.

3.17 The number of dioceses paying child allowances has also fallen, with only one diocese now paying these allowances. Historically, the CSA has encouraged dioceses not to pay these allowances, as it believed that it was better to increase stipends across the board for all clergy rather than target increases on one group. The case for child allowances is largely based on the assumption that the stipend is a living allowance.

3.18 Although the survey indicated that a majority of clergy support child allowances, and means testing for them, means testing is more difficult in practice than in theory: it raises difficult issues about how much additional income clergy should receive before qualifying for these payments; it will be time-consuming for diocesan offices to operate; and clergy are unlikely to be comfortable with applying for these allowances. Interestingly, in the one diocese that makes these payments, they are available to all clergy who apply for them.

3.19 If it is accepted that the stipend is payment for the exercise of office, then there is little justification for child allowances. The size of families remains primarily a decision for the couple involved. Supporting clergy families with large numbers of children is perhaps better done through the medium of clergy charities rather than by making additional payments to the stipend.

3.20 **We recommend that additional payments for children should not be made.**

3.21 From time to time, it is suggested that clergy in rural areas need to receive additional stipend payments. Not only is there the likelihood of higher official mileage in combined benefices, but local shops may charge higher prices and supermarkets may be a considerable distance away. There may be greater need for a second car, and it may be less easy for spouses to obtain jobs. Although these costs are arguably connected with employment, as clergy are required to live in the parish, the case for making these payments is not strong unless the stipend is regarded as a living allowance.

3.22 **We recommend, therefore, that additional payments should not be made to take into account the additional costs associated with living in rural areas.**

3.23 In Chapter 5 we develop proposals allowing greater diocesan flexibility in the setting of stipend levels. This would allow local decisions to be made as to the treatment of particularly demanding responsibilities.

clergy couples

3.24 There were 300 respondents or so to the survey who said that they were part of a clergy couple. Of this group, 151 people in clergy couples were both in parochial appointments. There were 111 cases where both partners received a full stipend. Although only 10 respondents indicated that they received no stipend, 40 clergy said that they shared one stipend. A further 42 clergy said that they were non-stipendiary due to the unavailability of posts. (Both partners in a clergy couple may have responded to the questionnaire. The results are therefore likely to include some double counting. The Review Group was aware of this possibility but did not wish to restrict the completion of the questionnaire to one partner in the marriage.)

3.25 There are a small number of clergy couples sharing one stipend. Proper reward for their stipendiary work should be given. This does not imply, however, that two houses or housing allowances should necessarily be made available, and the CSA's current guidelines for housing allowances specify that a housing allowance should not be payable in cases where clergy are married to clergy occupying an official residence.

3.26 **We recommend that full-time or part-time stipendiary clergy should receive an appropriate stipend for the post they occupy irrespective of whether their spouse is also stipendiary.**

(b) consultation document

3.27 Responses to the consultation document were wide-ranging and significant in their contribution to the group's deliberations. In the matter of level of stipend, views reflect the findings of the survey, namely that households experiencing greatest hardship consist of families with children who are dependent solely on the stipend.

3.28 Other significant points arising from the responses to the consultation document were as follows:

- One fifth of respondents said that the level of stipend was inadequate although a tiny minority of respondents expressed the view that it was adequate. One quarter said that there should be payments for special needs, most mentioning family situation, children or other dependants.

- A number of responses from lay people said that clergy stipends in some areas of the country were well in excess of average incomes in the locality. Other responses, however, reflected the belief that the clergy were underpaid. There were many examples given of individual cases of hardship, though it is neither possible nor even desirable for the group to comment on these or the reasons for them.

3.29 The main issues raised by both the survey and consultation process were as follows:

- **Debts**. A surprisingly high proportion of all respondents, over two-thirds (68%), stated that they had no debts. Nevertheless, a significant group, nearly one-third (32%), is therefore carrying varying levels of debt.

- **Erosion of savings**. Nearly two-fifths (38%) of all respondents to this question said that they had to draw on savings to meet normal living costs last year. However, nearly two-fifths (38%) of all respondents to a separate question said that they had added to their savings.

- **Financial gifts**. There is a high incidence of clergy receiving financial support from clergy or other charities, diocesan funds, family and friends, or parishioners. Even allowing for the fact that some families may have benefited from more that one grant, financial support is widespread. One charity that disbursed £683,000 to clergy in grants in 1999/2000 for the 'core' expenditure of holiday, welfare and school clothing stated that: 'This supports the view that we are making grants to a significant number of clergy for whom the current stipend is proving inadequate.'

- **Difficulties in meeting unplanned expenditure**. Among those respondents who have income in addition to stipend, three-fifths (61%) said that they struggled to pay bills or could pay all bills but could not afford other things. For those families reliant solely on their stipend, less than two-fifths (37%) expressed similar views.

- **Student loan repayments**. Concern was expressed that recent changes in the rules regarding the repayment of student loans mean that newly ordained assistant clergy will be faced with repaying student loans when they fall due in two years' time.

- **Other financially related pressures**. Views were expressed about costs of families attending parish functions and fundraising events especially in multi-parish benefices, costs of running large, sometimes not modernized, vicarages, the inadequacy of removal grants and the cost of furnishing large houses.

- **Stress on marriages and children** of the constant vigilance about money, and the pressures on children who could not share in the lifestyles of their peers. A significant number of married clergy appear to rely on the income of a spouse to augment the family income. Such reliance on a spouse's income should not influence consideration of the appropriate level of stipend. Similar pressures applied over the inability to afford leisure activities and holidays away from the vicarage.

- There appears some correlation between the **age of entering ministerial training** and financial adequacy. Over half (54%) of the survey respondents entered stipendiary ministry under 31 years of age and were less likely to have accumulated capital or chose to sell their house to finance their training. Those entering the ministry in mid-career are likely to have some financial reserves to supplement their stipend. While three-quarters (77%) of all respondents stated that they had some capital reserves, one-fifth (20%) said they did not.

● **Home ownership**. A significant group, nearly two-fifths (38%) of all respondents, own a residential property other than the one they live in. (Figures from Shelter indicate that, across the country, two-thirds (68%) of households are in owner occupation.) Mortgage payments are made by over half (53%) of all the homeowners and over half (52%) of the single stipend or low earner group. The proportion of clergy owning a property probably relates to the age profile of respondents where nearly two-thirds (65%) are aged 46 years and over and will be making long-term provision, or have inherited a property or retained their home on entering the ministry.

(c) comparison with other churches

3.30 Any comparison of stipends with other churches must take account of differing practices in the manner in which benefits other than stipend are treated, for example in the provision of housing, pensions and in two cases, a children's allowance. Ten church organizations in the United Kingdom provided details, while three churches overseas described their remuneration practices. Details are shown in **Appendix 5**.

3.31 Each church organization manages its affairs differently; for some, the level of stipend is determined centrally, while for others it is left to a local congregation. Where stipends are determined locally, comparisons are used such as Teachers or National Joint Council pay scales or representative income levels of church members.

3.32 Graded supplements are paid in the early years of ministry in three Church organizations while pension contributions of up to 6.5% of stipend are made by clergy in 5 of the 10 UK-based church organizations. The remainder, apart from one that has no formal pension arrangements, operate non-contributory schemes.

3.33   Levels of stipend for 2001 in other churches are summarized below.

Church	Incumbent	Assistant
Church of England	£16,040 (NMS) £16,910 (NSB)	£15,120 (year 1) £15,810 (year 4) (plus additional points for seniority and responsibility up to £16,920)
Methodist*	£14,940	
United Reformed*	£16,944 + £800 for first child, £400 for each additional child	
Baptist*	£14,600 (minimum)	
Roman Catholic*	Determined at diocesan level: See **Appendix 5**	
Church in Wales*	£16,705	£13,523
Church in Ireland*	£19,086	£14,315 (min) £16,725 (max after 5 years)
Episcopal Church of Scotland	As for Church of England	As for Church of England
Church of Scotland*	£22,182 (maximum after 5 years)	£18,016 (basic without service supplement)
Ichthus Christian Fellowship	£16,000 (maximum)	£13,000

*These clergy retain the fees, where given, unlike Church of England clergy, who either assign their fees to the diocese, or have their stipends adjusted to reflect the fees already received. Ministers in the Church of Scotland and the United Reformed Church do not charge fees to members of their congregation.

The level of stipend is effectively reduced where the church pension scheme is contributory. In those cases the adjusted stipend would be:

Methodist	£14,040
Baptist	£13,870
Ichthus Christian Fellowship	£15,200

Church of Scotland ministers also pay a compulsory contribution of 2% of the basic stipend (without service supplement) into a money purchase pension scheme. This applies to new entrants only.

3.34   In summary, the above comparisons give a varied picture of stipend levels. The current level of stipend for incumbents is positioned broadly in the middle. In the case of assistant staff, current levels of stipend compare favourably with those of other churches.

the value of the clergy remuneration package

3.35   Comparisons of clergy pay with other professional groups are not straightforward to make for reasons of the nature of their vocation, job type and level, employment basis, career and the absence of performance-linked pay progression, and the comparative lack of influence of market factors.

the value of provided housing

3.36   Ascribing a value to the benefits clergy receive is not easy. Nevertheless, the Group does believe that comparisons with other professions require a value to be given to provided housing. A methodology has been used by the Central Stipends Authority since 1980 (with revisions), and the results are published in the CSA's annual report to the General Synod. The calculation aims to provide a general indication of the amount of additional gross income which clergy of incumbent status would, on average, require in order to provide basic domestic accommodation (excluding office space) for themselves and their families. It is *not* intended to be an indication of the cost of providing accommodation for clergy, although it is used in some dioceses as the basis of a housing allowance in cases where clergy do own their own house.

3.37   One feature of this calculation is the use of rental costs rather than basing the calculation on ownership. It is often noted that clergy do not have the opportunity to benefit from increases in the value of the house which, were they not clergy, they would probably own. On the other hand, they are spared the cost of paying mortgage interest.

3.38   The existing methodology is also based on the costs related to an average semi-detached house. This is partly because this is seen as the kind of accommodation most likely to be affordable by those with the same disposable income as clergy. It also recognizes that, along with the benefits, there are some disadvantages to clergy in having their accommodation provided for them. These disadvantages are considered further at paragraph 3.44.

3.39   The Group noted the contrast between the semi-detached house on which the CSA's calculation was based and the current Church Commissioners' Green Guide standard of a four bedroom house (up to 2,050 square feet (190m^2) with study and garage, all in 0.10 to 0.25 acres (0.04 to 0.10 ha)). It is a fact that most lay people supporting the Church cannot afford to live in such houses. This is also a point of criticism among some clergy who feel the Church is wrong to provide houses for its clergy that are larger and more expensive than the housing stock in many parishes.

3.40 We therefore looked at figures which might be closer to the actual situation and more correctly reflect the value of the house provision – and have taken figures for owning, not renting, the average semi-detached and detached house in the UK. Our revised method brings these factors into play to provide a truer comparison with those who own their own houses. The nature of the housing market is that some periods witness large increases in house prices and much comment on the subject, which becomes more muted in periods when prices are set back. The long-term history has been for house prices to increase at some 1.5% above RPI. Our figures use this assumption for the future, assuming the RPI will average 2.5% and hence house prices will increase on average by 4% p.a.

Cost and Note number	CSA Report method £	Comparison using data on owner-occupied housing	
		Semi-detached £	**Detached** £
Average value of house	–	97,642	176,564
Rent (6% of average value of semi-detached house)	5,040	n/a	n/a
Mortgage interest (1)	n/a	6,835	12,359
Water charges (2)	233	233	233
Council Tax (3)	991	991	991
Maintenance and external decorations (4)	423	423	423
Insurance (5)	71	82	149
Cost of changing house (6)	0	1,145	1,656
(less average gain in house prices) (7)	0	(3,905)	(7,062)
Sub total	6,758	5,804	8,749
Tax and National Insurance adjustment (8)	2,952	2,535	3,821
Total	**£9,710**	**£8,339**	**£12,570**

(1) Interest at 7.0% (4.5% above inflation at 2.5%) on the full cost of a house priced at £97,642/£176,564. No allowances for repayment of capital. The figures for house prices shown are taken from data available from the Valuation Office Agency's Property Market Report. The CSA method uses figures for house prices from the Nationwide Building Society.
(2) OFWAT figures for average water and sewerage charges.
(3) Average clergy Council Tax from the 1997 questionnaire, increased in line with estimates from the Department of Transport, Local Government and the Regions.
(4) 2000 figure (based on government statistics for average household expenditure in respect of repairs, maintenance and decoration derived from the Family Expenditure Survey) increased by RPI (repairs and maintenance charges element).
(5) 2000 average premium for each type of house in England, excluding Church discount and including 5% Insurance Premium Tax. (Data provided by the EIG.)
(6) Includes (for house of two values £97,642/£176,564), stamp duty (£976/£1,766), legal costs on purchase and sale (£1,147/£2,075), agent's sale fee (£2,295/£4,149), moving costs (£2,000) and resettlement costs in line with the CSA minimum scale (£1,600), a total of £8,018/£11,590. These costs are then divided by seven on the assumption that a house move takes place every seven years.
(7) Estimated at 4% p.a. as indicated above.
(8) Tax at basic rate of 22% and National Insurance at the marginal rate of 8.4%.

3.41 The figures include an allowance for other elements of the remuneration package such as Council Tax paid for by the Church on behalf of the clergy. This, we believe, shows more clearly than before the net benefit of providing housing to our clergy, and, taking account of the apparent advantage of increasing equity, we think this comparison is truer than the one used at present.

3.42 The national average figures used in this calculation inevitably do not reflect individual circumstances or the considerable variation in house prices over the country, as well as across individual dioceses. In 2000, the average cost of a typical new parsonage (including land costs) in Guildford Diocese was between £375,000 and £450,000, whilst in Newcastle it was around £145,000. However, the figure of £12,570 p.a shown above is a measure of the absolute minimum extra sum the Church would have to pay in stipend to allow an incumbent to provide housing of a standard similar to that currently recommended in the Green Guide.

3.43 Any value attached to the net benefit of tied housing can only be an approximation. Some members of the Group consider that the value we have used understates the reality for a 'Green Guide' standard benefice house.

3.44 Although the new methodology does take into account the fact that clergy, by virtue of having their housing provided for them, are not able to take advantage of capital growth in the value of housing, there are other disadvantages to clergy in having their housing provided. These are also discussed in Chapter 7, and include the following:

- Clergy have no unfettered choice of where to live or the kind of housing provided for them.
- Clergy have concerns about the cost of housing themselves in retirement.
- The housing is probably larger than clergy would choose and attracts higher bills for heating.
- Part of their house is used for work purposes, and is effectively not part of the home. The Inland Revenue assesses this at 25% of the whole, when agreeing the proportion of expenditure on Heating, Lighting and Cleaning that is paid tax free.
- There is an expectation of constant availability.

3.45 The Group agrees that these disadvantages need to be taken into account when assessing the value of provided housing. It believes that the value of provided accommodation should be assessed on the basis of detached owner-occupied housing shown above (£12,570) with a deduction of 25% to reflect the disadvantages. A figure of £9,428 would result from the calculations above. **We recommend the use of this methodology to the Archbishops' Council as Central Stipends Authority for use in future.**

(d) comparisons with other professions

3.46 On the basis of the calculation above, the value of provided accommodation in 2001 is £9,428. Adding this figure to the National Stipend Benchmark in 2001/02 of £16,910 gives a notional value to the clergy remuneration package in 2001 of £26,338.

3.47 The following groups have earnings at about this level.

Primary School teaching professionals	£25,330
Town planners	£26,340
Midwives	£25,260
Environmental Health officers	£25,300
Estimators, valuers	£25,850
Average all non-manual occupations	£25,570

(New Earnings Survey 2000 uprated by AEI at April 2001)

3.48 It is clear that the work and levels of responsibility of these groups do not necessarily resemble those of the clergy. The Group also regarded some of the comparisons that have been made in the past as not appropriate (for example, charity and social workers, and probation officers).

3.49 The Group also noted Incomes Data Services' analysis of the distribution of earnings, using the New Earnings Survey data for April 2000, which indicated that over half of all full-time employees were paid between £10,000 and £20,000 p.a. Median earnings, the level at which half of people earned more and half less, were £18,200 a year. Most people earned below the average level of earnings of £21,370 p.a.

3.50 The Group is of the opinion that the following professions might be considered to have similar levels of responsibility or status within the community to clergy.

GP (net of practice costs)	£54,890*
Primary School Headteacher (starting point)	£36,471
Accountant (employee average from NES)	£32,920
Solicitor (employee average from NES)	£42,520
Civil Servant (Archbishops' Council Senior Executive Officer mid-point)	£28,862

(*New Earnings Survey 2000 uprated by AEI at April 2001)

3.51 This means that the following initial conclusions can be drawn when comparing clergy remuneration with other professions:

- The level of clergy remuneration appears to be equal to that of those doing dissimilar work.
- It is slightly above the national average non-manual wage.
- Those engaged in similar kinds of work receive remuneration often at a considerably higher level than clergy.
- Clergy remuneration is above the earnings of more than half the population.

3.52 The Group noted that the Civil Service Senior Executive Officer (SEO) grade is used for most clergy who work for the Archbishops' Council, even though the work of these clergy is of a different kind from that done by parochial clergy. The Group considers, however, that the closest approximation to the role of an incumbent is the primary school headteacher who, like parochial clergy, is charged with representing an institution within the community, although the analogy is not appropriate in all respects. Like headteachers, clergy have a leadership role within their parishes, and are required to respond to the pastoral needs of those in their care. Clergy are required to inspire and challenge their congregations to realize the full potential to which God has called them. They have to ensure that parish resources are properly managed, and are responsible for motivating and enabling groups of volunteers and, in some cases, paid employees.

3.53 We consider, however, that it is important to give sufficient weight to the sacrificial element of the vocation to ordained stipendiary ministry. Nor should it be assumed, simply because the responsibilities of clergy may resemble those of a headteacher, that the level of remuneration should automatically be identical.

3.54 **We therefore recommend that the appropriate point of comparison for an incumbent's remuneration (that is, stipend and housing) should be approximately 80% of the starting salary of the head teacher of a large primary school.**

3.55 We have examined the pay scales appropriate for a headteacher of a large (480 pupils) primary school. As at September 2000, there was a twelve-point scale between £36,471 and £47,703. On the assumption that the National Stipend Benchmark is payable to a newly appointed incumbent, the direct point of comparison would appear to be with the start of this scale.

3.56 This suggests that the appropriate stipend for incumbents in 2001/02 would be as follows:

80% of starting point of headteacher scale	£29,176
Value of clergy housing	(£9,428)
Appropriate stipend for incumbents	£19,748

Accordingly, reflecting on the range of considerations, the Group recommends £20,000 as the appropriate stipend for incumbents.

3.57 The National Stipend Benchmark is currently 1.05 of the National Minimum Stipend. On the assumption that this relationship is preserved, this would have produced a National Minimum Stipend of £19,050. However, Chapter 5 goes on to consider the recommendation that the National Stipend Benchmark should be 1.1 of the NMS. If this recommendation had already been in force, then the 2001/02 NMS would have been £18,180, say £18,200.

3.58 Given the current figures of £16,910 (NSB) and £16,040 (NMS), it is clear that the Church is not in a position to realize the aspiration of 80% of the starting salary of the head teacher of a large primary school immediately. However, we commend it to the Church as an ideal to be aimed for. Issues of affordability are explored in Chapter 10.

3.59 We note that the figure of £20,000 fits quite well with the responses to the clergy survey, where the most popular option (supported by over one-quarter (28%) of respondents) was that a reasonable stipend would be between £19,000 and £21,000.

3.60 We also note that this figure approaches that suggested by clergy members of the MSF Union, who suggested that the appropriate stipend level for incumbents was that currently paid to residentiary canons (£20,800 in 2001/02).

chapter 4

the concept and level of differentials

4.1 The subject of the place of differentials within the remuneration of the clergy is one that is regularly raised and can produce impassioned debate. The alternative points of view expressed were reflected both in our survey of clergy and in the evidence submitted to us. The Group has reflected very carefully on the issues before it. The concept of differentials and the level at which they are set are, of course, closely related to the theological principles that are used to underpin the understanding of stipend in Chapter 2.

4.2 Differentials have been a feature of clergy stipends throughout the history of the Church of England. At one stage they were far greater than they are today. In 1835 the Archbishop of Canterbury's stipend was 65 times that of an average incumbent, and a diocesan bishop's 16 times. Disparities between incumbents' stipends were also sometimes very large, often bearing little relationship to the levels of work required in serving the parishes concerned.

4.3 Moves over the last two centuries have gradually eroded those differentials. By 1939 the ratio of a diocesan bishop's stipend to an average incumbent's stipend had reduced to 6 to 1, and today it is 1.84 to 1. Differences between incumbents' stipends have been largely removed.

4.4 Our terms of reference required us to examine the levels of differentials but not their principle. However the evidence from our surveys indicates a substantial body of opinion in the Church, albeit a minority opinion, that would like to see the abolition or at least a very substantial lessening of differentials. We gave some consideration to this issue, noting three matters in the relatively recent history of the Church:

- *Differentials: A Report to the General Synod by the Central Stipends Authority*, 1977 (GS 333);
- The General Synod debate on differentials in February 1996;
- The survey of stipendiary clergy and lay workers undertaken as part of the current review.

the 1977 Differentials Report (GS 333)

4.5   In 1975 the General Synod invited the Central Stipends Authority to 'institute an enquiry into the need and justification for differentials in basic stipends between full-time servants of the Church'. A working party under the chairmanship of the then Bishop of Ripon (the Rt Revd S. Hetley Price) was established, and, as in the 1975 debate some people had questioned the very existence of differentials, they were represented on the working party.

4.6   The arguments against and for differentials were summarized as follows:

against the maintenance of differentials

i)   The payment of the clergy should demonstrably be based upon the gospel, which cannot be held to support a differential pay structure for those directly engaged with the cure of souls.

ii)   Remuneration should be related as closely as possible to the needs of a clergyman having particular regard to the expenses of his ministry and his domestic and social responsibilities.

iii)   Society at large needs some sort of graphic demonstration or example from the Church and one such example would be given if the payment of the clergy were to be related to their needs rather than to the post they held or the responsibilities they carried.

iv)   The fellowship of the clergy would be strengthened if all were thought of as carrying similar responsibilities and seen to be receiving similar financial rewards.

v)   As between incumbents it would be impossible fairly to evaluate their responsibilities and a wholly equitable structure of differentials would therefore be unattainable.

arguments for differentials

i)   Different levels of responsibility are rightly reflected in different stipend levels not only as a recognition of the duties of the post, but also because different levels of responsibility entail different patterns of expenditure, which cannot adequately be catered for either by a system of allowances or by reimbursement of working expenses in a strict sense.

ii)   The clergy are not immune from the general desire for a fair reward relating to work done and it is wrong to legislate as though they were.

iii) The Church of England is an institution set in the world and has a married clergy. It has close links with the life of the nation and it cannot contract out of the financial system of the society in which it exists.

iv) Differentials have been very substantially reduced over the years and further reduction is not called for by any principle of equity.

v) Elaborate expenses accounts or allowance systems are difficult to frame equitably and are open to abuse. It is better to give a man a larger stipend to spend at his own discretion than to pay him a smaller stipend with additional payments directed towards meeting specific needs.

4.7 The report then turned to matters of principle. R.H. Tawney in *Religion and the Rise of Capitalism*, was quoted:

> There are, perhaps, four main attitudes which religious opinion may adopt towards the world of social institutions and economic relations. It may stand on one side in ascetic aloofness and regard them as in their nature the sphere of unrighteousness, from which men may escape – but which they can conquer only by flight. It may take them for granted and ignore them, as matters of indifference belonging to a world with which religion has no concern; in all ages the procedure of looking problems boldly in the face and passing on has seemed too self-evident to require justification. It may throw itself into an agitation for some particular reform, for the removal of some crying scandal, for the promotion of some final solution, which will inaugurate the reign of righteousness on earth. It may at once accept and criticise, tolerate and amend, welcome the gross world of human appetites as squalid scaffolding from amid which the life of the spirit must arise, and insist that this also is the material of the Kingdom of God. (pp 32–3 of the Pelican edition.)

4.8 The 1977 Report suggested three responses to differentials in the light of that analysis:

i) There should be no differentials, they are part of 'the sphere of unrighteousness' which can be conquered only by flight.

ii) Differentials should be a matter of indifference, belonging to a world with which religion has no real concern, and therefore they may be accepted without very much thought or argument.

iii) 'The gross world of human appetites' should be welcomed as the rough material from which the kingdom has to be built. We should be therefore be ready to work within a system of differentials but it should be a system which would not be extravagant and which could be assessed according to practicable and generally acceptable criteria.

4.9 In accepting, in practice, the third response, the 1977 Differentials Report considered the biblical evidence, and particularly 1 Timothy 5.17: 'Elders who do well as leaders should be reckoned worthy of a double stipend, in particular those who labour at preaching and teaching.' The report noted the scholarly debate about the meaning of the Greek word *time* translated stipend, but concluded that most commentators accepted that it indicated some financial consideration. It also recognized that there was likely to be a variety of practices in the emerging ministry of the Church in New Testament times and that it was impossible to extract precise instructions from the New Testament and apply them without question in any age of the church.

4.10 The report then noted the tension between the Church being both a sign of the kingdom and an institution within the context of the society in which it lives. These issues are explored further in Chapter 2. As a sign of the kingdom, any differentials might be related to need, but as an institution within society the report noted that many other institutions considered the use of differentials to reflect both different levels of responsibility and achievement to be ethically reasonable. It also noted that many lay servants of the church employed in administrative roles were paid on such a basis.

4.11 In that section of the report the first conclusion was that from the biblical evidence and from theological and ethical principles it was not possible to draw a single unassailable conclusion. However, the report's final conclusion is worth noting in full:

> While Christian teaching has much to say about inordinate desires, there are also such things as ordinate desires legitimate for the individual in the satisfaction they provide both for himself and in the provision he may make for his family, and not hostile to the good life of the fellowship. While gross inequalities may wreck the fellowship, modest differences may help a society called to live the difficult life implicit in any attempt to work out in practice the implications of an incarnational theology – a body of people representative of fallen humanity who are yet called to partake of the divine nature.

The majority of the working party concluded that the diminution of differentials had in general gone far enough. Their view was subsequently endorsed by the General Synod.

the 1996 General Synod debate

4.12 In February 1996 the General Synod debated a motion from the Carlisle Diocesan Synod calling for the abolition of differentials. A background paper from the Clergy Conditions of Service Steering

Group included some earlier material, including the relevant chapters from the 1977 Report. A full two-hour debate gave opportunity for many points of view to be expressed. The motion to abolish differentials was eventually *lost* in all three houses, with particular support for differentials from the House of Laity.

	Ayes	Noes
Bishops	4	16
Clergy	77	89
Laity	68	105

the current survey

4.13 As part of the process of this current review a survey of all stipendiary clergy and licensed lay workers on the central payroll was undertaken. One of the questions was 'Do you agree with the principle of differentials?.' 53% agreed or strongly agreed. 42% disagreed or strongly disagreed.

4.14 Those 53% who agreed were then asked whether differentials should be paid to different roles. The responses were:

Role	YES	NO	Not answered
Diocesan Bishops	94%	2%	3%
Suffragan Bishops	92%	4%	4%
Deans/Provosts	69%	25%	6%
Archdeacons	82%	13%	4%
Residentiary Canons	28%	64%	8%
Area/Rural Deans	53%	42%	6%

4.15 The responses to further questions asked about differentials for other positions were:

Role	YES	NO	Not answered
Demanding parochial jobs	34%	63%	2%
Diocesan roles held with parochial responsibilities	27%	71%	2%
Clergy with entirely diocesan responsibilities	4%	94%	2%

4.16 On differentials between incumbents and assistant staff and licensed lay workers, respondents were asked to state whether they agreed with four statements:

Assistant staff and licensed layworkers should ...	YES	NO	Not answered
receive at least the same as the NMS for incumbents	66%	31%	3%
receive the same stipend as incumbents	38%	57%	5%
be on a progressive scale	68%	27%	6%
all receive the same	53%	41%	6%

4.17 The survey therefore indicates considerable variations of opinion in the Church on these matters. There is majority acceptance of the principle of differentials, particularly for bishops, deans and archdeacons, less support for differentials for rural/area deans, and even less for residentiary canons, or within parochial ministry. There is general support for a progressive scale for assistant staff and a small majority in favour of the same scales being used for licensed lay workers as for assistant ordained staff.

4.18 **Our conclusion is to accept the arguments of the 1977 Differentials Report, the voting in the 1996 General Synod debate and the evidence of the responses to our survey of stipendiary clergy. We believe that some modest differentials in clergy pay are both theologically reasonable and generally acceptable in the Church of England.**

current levels of differentials

4.19 The differentials structure in the stipend year 2001/02 is as follows:

	Stipend	Multiple of National Minimum Stipend
Assistant Staff (year 1)	£15,120	0.94
Assistant Staff (year 2)	£15,370	0.96
Assistant Staff (year 3)	£15,590	0.97
Assistant Staff (year 4)	£15,810	0.99
National Minimum Stipend	£16,040	–
Assistant Staff A	£16,050	1
Assistant Staff B	£16,290	1.02
Incumbent NSB	£16,910	1.05
Residentiary Canon	£20,800	1.30
Archdeacon	£25,370	1.58
Dean/Suffragan Bishop	£25,530	1.59
Diocesan Bishop	£31,110	1.94
Bishop of London	£46,840	2.92
Archbishop of York	£50.220	3.13
Archbishop of Canterbury	£57,320	3.57

We have noted that in many dioceses the residentiary canon's scale is used for other diocesan roles and that other lesser differentials are used for other posts including, in some cases, rural deans. There appears to be no overall consistency between dioceses in the use of other differentials.

4.20 The Church of England exists in a society where differentials are commonplace. Differentials are normally calculated on the basis of qualifications, performance or levels of responsibility, or some combination of all three.

4.21 We see no good reason for paying clergy because they hold additional qualifications; ordination itself is the critical 'qualification'. We also believe performance-related pay is impracticable in relation to ministry. What would constitute 'good' performance? How are 'faithfulness', 'prayer' or other spiritual matters to be measured? The independence of the preacher to speak the truth of the gospel clearly, however uncomfortable it may be to the local congregation, is an important, and immeasurable concept. We do, however, believe that some financial recognition of different levels of responsibility is compatible with Scripture, theology and ethics.

4.22 While the range of differentials in some secular areas may seem extreme, we note that in many other areas they are widely accepted. Indeed as the 1977 report noted many lay people employed by the Church are used to working in such a context. We noted four particular relevant areas:

- Schools
- Charities
- Military Chaplains
- Staff of the Archbishops' Council.

schools

4.23 The differentials in schools (including church schools) vary depending on the size of school. Some discretion is also given to governors, but the Department for Education and Skills provides guidance for all school teachers' salaries. The differentials we have selected for the purposes of comparison are: starting salary for a teacher with a good honours degree; a teacher on the first point of the upper pay scale with one management point and two recruitment and retention points (traditionally used by the CSA for comparison with incumbents' stipends); a primary school headteacher at the start of the scale; and the starting point of the scale for a headteacher of a secondary school of 1,500 (chosen because it will employ slightly fewer staff than a medium-sized diocese will have stipendiary clergy).

charities

4.24 The Reward Group publishes a very thorough survey of salaries paid by charities. In their edition for 1999/2000, they give a seven-point scale of management roles. At each level there will be considerable variations in pay according to the circumstances and size of different charities, but the Reward Group give the median figure for each level. The CSA considers an incumbent's level of responsibility is roughly equivalent to the middle management level. Differentials in the table below are given in relation to salaries in management positions.

military chaplains

4.25 Army, Royal Navy and Royal Air Force Chaplains are paid on a common scale, with increments for every two years of service. As very few serve titles as a military chaplain, the first appointment could be seen as equivalent to the current NMS. It could also be argued that the differential received after four years' service is equivalent to an incumbency. An Anglican appointed as Chaplain-General is designated an Archdeacon.

staff of the Archbishops' Council

4.26 The mid-points of the Archbishops' Council staff scales as at 1 July 2000 are given. These figures include London Weighting and Local Pay Additions (where paid). The Higher Executive Officer (HEO) is taken as equivalent to a curate's post. The Senior Executive Officer (SEO) is taken as equivalent to an incumbent's post. The Senior Principal is taken as equivalent to an archdeacon's post. Senior Band 6 is the highest level on the scale for staff of the Archbishops' Council.

4.27 Differentials in each of the organizations mentioned above are given on the next page.

conclusions

4.28 As will be evident, the range of differentials in clergy stipends is modest compared to the ranges paid in those four areas. Purely for the purposes of looking at differentials, it does not seem unreasonable to compare a diocesan bishop to a chaplain-general, a chief executive

Schools		Charities		Military Chaplains		Staff of the Archbishops' Council	
	Salary	Multiple		Salary	Multiple		Salary	Multiple		Salary	Multiple

Schools			Charities			Military Chaplains			Staff of the Archbishops' Council		
	Salary	Multiple		Salary	Multiple		Salary	Multiple		Salary	Multiple
Starting salary	£16,050	1	Trainee Manager	£17,475	1	On appointment	£27,784	1	HEO	£23,743	1
First point on upper pay scale*	£29,332	1.83	Junior Manager	20,062	1.15	After 4 years*	£31,813	1.15	SEO*	£28,862	1.22
Primary School Head	£36,471	2.27	Middle Manager*	£23,691	1.36	Principal Chaplain	£57,170	2.06	Senior Principal	£43,798	1.84
Mid point of scale for Secondary School Head	£55,254	3.44	Senior Manager	£27,255	1.56	Deputy Chaplain General	£60,178	2.16	Senior band 3	£68,511	2.89
			Head of Function	£32,393	1.85	Chaplain General	£69,828	2.51	Senior band 6	£88,026	3.71
			Other Directors	£42,090	2.41						
			Chief Executive	£50,470	2.89						

* denotes post considered equivalent to incumbent

of a medium-sized charity, the headteacher of a secondary school of
1,500 or at least Band 3 in the civil service range. The National
Minimum Stipend can be compared to teachers, trainee charity
managers at the start of their careers, military chaplains on
appointment or HEOs. The comparisons of differentials are:

Diocesan Bishop	1.84 times	NMS
Primary Headteacher	2.27 times	teacher's starting salary
Secondary Headteacher	3.44 times	teacher's starting salary
Charity Chief Executive	2.89 times	trainee manager's salary
Chaplain-General	2.51 times	chaplain on appointment
Civil Service Band 3	2.89 times	Higher Executive Officer

4.29 As the remuneration for some of these posts is likely to be provided
by a church or Christian body, these figures could, therefore, be taken
as an argument for increasing rather than diminishing differentials
within the Church. However we recognize that such a policy is unlikely
to commend itself to the General Synod or the wider Church. **We do,
however, recommend that the basic range of differentials in the
church should not be further diminished.**

specific recommendations

4.30 **Archdeacons, deans, suffragan and area bishops.** We believe the
current differential between Suffragan or Area Bishops and Cathedral
Deans on the one hand and Archdeacons on the other hand is so
small (£160 p.a.) as to be meaningless. There is a strong case for
seeing the responsibilities of suffragan or area bishops and deans as
being comparable, but recognizing that the public role of archdeacons
is less. **We therefore recommend that the absence of a
differential between deans on the one hand and suffragan and
area bishops on the other should be maintained. We also
recommend that the differential with archdeacons should be
increased, so archdeacons should receive a stipend of
1.6 times the NMS (currently 1.58 of the NMS) and deans,
suffragan and area bishops should receive a stipend of
1.7 times the NMS (currently 1.59 of the NMS).**

4.31 Bishops receive relatively small differentials given the additional levels
of responsibility they bear. We believe there may be a case for
substantially increasing their differentials but do not believe this is the
moment for making such a change. **For the sake of simplicity we
recommend moving the present stipend of 1.94 of the NMS
to 2 times the NMS.**

4.32 **Higher Differentials.** It is clear that the Bishop of London has greater responsibilities than many diocesan bishops, partly because of the size of his diocese, but also because of the specific national responsibilities that fall on the Bishop of the nation's capital. At present his stipend is 1.5 times a diocesan bishop's stipend, or 2.92 of the NMS. **We recommend moving the present differential of 2.92 to 3.0 of the NMS.**

4.33 Equally the two Archbishops have further additional responsibilities. The stipend for the Archbishop of York is 1.61 times a diocesan bishop's stipend, or 3.13 of the NMS. The stipend for the Archbishop of Canterbury is 1.84 times a diocesan bishop's stipend or 3.57 of the NMS. That is a slightly lesser differential than the salary of a headteacher of a secondary school of 1,500 earning 4.08 times the starting salary of a teacher with a good honours degree. Given a system of differentials we believe those additional responsibilities merit greater stipends. **We recommend adjusting the stipend for the Archbishop of York from 3.13 to 3.25 of the NMS and that for the Archbishop of Canterbury from 3.57 to 3.75 of the NMS.**

4.34 **The recommended changes to the differentials structure are summarized below.**

	Current stipend (multiple of NMS)	**New differential** (multiple of NMS)
Residentiary Canon	1.30	–
Archdeacon	1.58	**1.6**
Dean/Suffragan Bishop	1.59	**1.7**
Diocesan Bishop	1.94	**2**
Bishop of London	2.92	**3**
Archbishop of York	3.13	**3.25**
Archbishop of Canterbury	3.57	**3.75**

chapter 5
a new stipends system

the current system

5.1   The current stipends system came into place in 1998 in response to
dioceses' concerns that stipend levels in dioceses were moving too far
apart. Details of the current recommendations made by the Central
Stipends Authority each year are provided at **Appendix 4**. The
process of setting stipends and the role of the Central Stipends
Authority are considered in Chapter 6.

5.2   Features to be noted about the current system are as follows:

   i) The only stipends currently adjusted for regional variations are
   those of incumbents.

   ii) The system, whilst encouraging stipend convergence, provides for
   diocesan flexibility by asking dioceses to ensure that the stipend
   paid to the greatest number of incumbents in the diocese (the
   Diocesan Basic Stipend) is neither 1.5% below nor above 2.5% of
   the Diocesan Regional Stipend Benchmarks.

   iii) No upper limit is given for stipends paid to clergy of incumbent
   status. In practice, however, most differential payments stop at
   the level of the residentiary canon's stipend.

   iv) The CSA's recommendations take account of diocesan voting for
   their preferred increase in the CSA's recommendations, but the
   actual level of stipend paid in a dioceses remains for the diocese
   to decide.

5.3   There is general adherence to the CSA's recommendations, but the
following points should be noted:

   i) The national average stipend for incumbents in 2001/02 was
   £120 higher than the National Stipend Benchmark

   ii) Many dioceses do not follow the scale for assistant staff.

   iii) In the year 2001/02, two dioceses paid a basic stipend that was
   more than 2.5% above their RSB, and two dioceses paid less
   than 1.5% below their RSB.

iv) The Church Commissioners have agreed to follow the CSA's recommendations in setting stipends for bishops, deans and residentiary canons.

5.4 Among the issues raised by the survey of stipendiary clergy and lay workers were the following:

i) Two-thirds (65%) of respondents agreed/strongly agreed that assistant staff and licensed lay workers should receive at least the National Minimum Stipend for incumbents.

ii) Two-thirds (66%) disagreed/strongly disagreed that assistant staff should receive the same stipend as incumbents.

iii) Over two-thirds (68%) agreed/strongly agreed that assistant staff should be on a progressive stipend scale for the first 4 years with additional points for responsibility, but over half (53%) agreed/ strongly agreed that they should all receive the same stipend.

iv) There were conflicting messages about differentials between incumbencies.

v) Of those who declared themselves in favour of differentials, there was a majority in favour of some differential for rural/area deans (53% in favour, 42% against). No recommendations are currently made by the CSA about such differentials.

5.5 Other issues that came up in the Group's discussions included the following:

i) The current emphasis on the National Stipend Benchmark and the National Minimum Stipend for incumbents means that assistant staff are seen as receiving less than a full stipend.

ii) There appears from the survey to be some sympathy for a graduated scale for assistant staff, provided the minimum starting figure is no less than the National Minimum Stipend for incumbents.

iii) There is considerable variation in the extent to which dioceses apply differentials for diocesan posts. This partly reflects the fact that responsibilities will vary from diocese to diocese for the same post.

iv) It would be inappropriate for any recommendations to be too prescriptive, especially as an ever-increasing proportion of the stipends/pension bill is borne by parishes and dioceses. In view of this, it would be better for the CSA not to recommend specific differentials, e.g. for rural/area deans, since the nature and extent of these responsibilities tend to vary from diocese to diocese. Instead we believe it would be better to provide ranges within which dioceses can come to their own views on stipend levels.

v) Some parochial posts are at least at the level of responsibility of some residentiary canons. We have also observed that there is a wide variety of practice in the dioceses relating to using the residentiary canon's scale for other diocesan appointments.

5.6 These considerations, plus those in Chapter 3, suggest that the following areas of the current system could be improved:

i) There should be an increase in the CSA's recommended level for assistant staff, partly to reflect the fact that many dioceses are not using the current scale, and partly because these will be the clergy who will be finding it most difficult to manage financially.

ii) If the increase for assistant staff is implemented, there should also be an increase in the level of stipend for incumbents in relation to the NMS.

iii) There are currently no ceilings on differentials for clergy paid by dioceses, but it might be desirable to introduce them, as long as an element of flexibility is preserved and the CSA's recommendations are not unduly prescriptive.

iv) Producing an integrated stipend system that could accommodate residentiary canons within the stipend recommendations for parochial and diocesan clergy would be desirable.

a new system

5.7 **In view of these factors, we recommend the following.**

i) **As recommended in Chapter 3, the National Minimum Stipend for incumbents should become the minimum stipend for all clergy.** This would have the following advantages:

- It would improve the income of those who received the lowest stipends and were most likely to find the stipend inadequate.

- It would retain the National Minimum Stipend as the base used to calculate pensions.

ii) **The CSA should not recommend a detailed scale for assistant staff, particularly as many dioceses already use their own scales. Instead, it should recommend a range for assistant staff between the National Minimum Stipend for all clergy and 1.1 of the National Minimum Stipend, and encourage dioceses to determine where on the scale to pay their assistant staff.**

iii) **All of the CSA's recommendations should be expressed as multiples of the National Minimum Stipend.**

iv) **There should be an Incumbent's Stipend Guideline (ISG). This should be set at 1.1 of the NMS, rather than the 1.05 of the NMS at which the NSB is currently set.**

v) **The CSA should offer guidance about regional adjustments for the ISG.**

vi) **In order to allow dioceses a degree of flexibility, including differential payments to a limited number of their clergy, the CSA recommendations should specify a ceiling below which at least 80% of clergy in the diocese should be paid.**

vii) **There should be a further ceiling for all clergy of incumbent status, which would act as a maximum stipend.**

5.8 The Group was, however, not able to reach complete agreement on the following issues:

- **How high the ceilings for differentials (in (vi) and (vii) above) needed to be in relation to the NMS.** Some members were concerned that a high ceiling in relation to the NMS would give so much flexibility to dioceses in setting stipends that little sense of stipends coherence across the Church would remain. Other members argued for maximum flexibility in setting stipends. They also noted that there was already considerable variation across dioceses and a high ceiling would be more likely to persuade dioceses tempted to go outside the national framework to remain within it.

- **Whether the ceilings for differentials should be adjusted for regional variations in the cost of living, or be absolute figures that should apply across the whole country.** Members who wanted a high ceiling in relation to the NMS argued that there would be no need for formal regional adjustments to stipends because the range would be wide enough to accommodate regional variations in the cost of living between dioceses. Those members who wanted a lower ceiling in relation to the NMS argued that regionalization would go a long way to compensating for the narrower range and had the advantage of ensuring that all dioceses had the same degree of flexibility in setting stipends.

- **Whether the ceilings for differentials should incorporate residentiary canons.** The aim of members arguing for a higher ceiling was to include the stipends paid to residentiary canons within the range of stipends paid to all clergy of incumbent status. Those who preferred a lower ceiling also said that this was desirable but not, in their view, essential.

5.9 Models can be constructed using different ceilings for differentials. They can also be adjusted for regional variations in the cost of living. Two of the possible models are provided below and attention is given to their advantages and disadvantages.

5.10 Many features of these models are identical.

- The base of the range for stipends of assistant staff would be increased up to the level of the current National Minimum Stipend for incumbents.

- An Incumbent Stipend Guideline (ISG) would be set at 1.1 of the National Minimum Stipend.

- A ceiling would be set for the stipend paid to at least 80% of incumbent status clergy in a diocese.

- A further ceiling would be set for the stipend paid to no more than 20% of incumbent status clergy in a diocese.

5.11 A model with regional variations

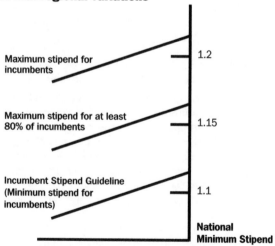

5.12 The features of this model are as follows:

- No adjustment is made to the NMS for regional variations in the cost of living.

- Stipends for clergy of incumbent status fall within the range of 1.1–1.2 of the NMS regionally adjusted.

- The ISG and the differential ceilings are adjusted for regional variations in the cost of living, and no one of incumbent status would be paid less than the regionally adjusted ISG, other than in exceptional circumstances.

- At least 80% of incumbent status clergy within a diocese could be paid within a range between 1.1 and 1.15 of NMS. (That is, no more than 20% of incumbent status clergy in a diocese would be paid more than 5% of the NMS above the ISG.

- No more than 20% of clergy within a diocese could be paid within a range between 1.15 and 1.2 of NMS. (That is, no clergy of incumbent status would be paid more than 10% of the NMS above the ISG.)

- On the figures proposed in Chapter 3, this model would use an NMS of £18,200, an ISG of £20,000 and ceilings of £20,900 (below which at least 80% of incumbent status clergy should be paid) and £21,800 (the maximum ceiling for stipends for clergy of incumbent status), all figures apart from the NMS being regionally adjusted.

5.13 The advantages of this model are:

- This proposal is similar in many ways to the existing stipends regional benchmark system.

- It takes fully into account the markedly different living costs in the North of England and in the South Eastern counties.

- It will be seen as a fair system, as it provides the same extent of flexibility to all dioceses, once the effects of regional variations in the cost of living are taken into account.

- The margins are widened to give dioceses more scope for internal differential payments, and the ability to progress in improving stipends at their own pace.

- It presents a manageable challenge to improve stipends, which most dioceses might be able to achieve once the effects of the revised pension contribution rates have been assimilated.

- It produces a greater degree of stipend convergence and sense of national coherence than the fixed range model with higher ceilings which is described below.

5.14   The potential disadvantages of this model are as follows:

- It may not encompass principals of colleges and courses (where the Lichfield Scale recommends that they are paid at the same level as residentiary canons), directors of education, and other posts paid at the same level as residentiary canons. As a result, incumbents of major parishes would either be seen as having a 'lesser' role than the holders of these posts, or it would be necessary to reduce the stipends paid to such clergy for new appointments to bring them into line with those paid to incumbents.

- There is a considerable jump from the top of the incumbent scale (1.2 times the NMS) and next level of differential for archdeacons (1.6 times the NMS).

- The ceiling for at least 80% of diocesan clergy is likely to be below what some dioceses wish to pay the majority of incumbents in 2002/3, and will leave many dioceses 'outside the system'.

- By not encompassing the whole of the Church of England, it could lead to many years of each diocese doing 'what is right in its own eyes', and would weaken the sense of being a national church.

- It results in a more complex system than the fixed range model (see below).

5.15   A fixed range model

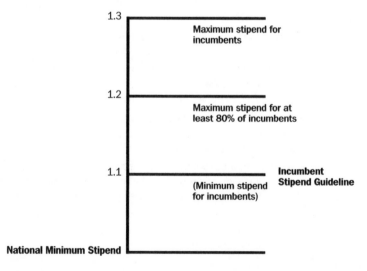

5.16 The features of this model are as follows:

- No full-time incumbent should receive less than the ISG.
- Figures for regional variations in the cost of living would be provided only as a guide.
- Dioceses would set their stipends for at least 80% of incumbents and incumbent status clergy within a range between 1.1 and 1.2 times the NMS (not regionalized).
- Dioceses would set their stipends for no more than 20% of incumbents and incumbent status clergy within a range between 1.2 and 1.3 times the NMS (not regionalized).
- On the figures proposed in Chapter 3, this model would have an NMS of £18,200, an ISG of £20,000 and ceilings of £21,800 (below which at least 80% of incumbent status clergy should be paid) and £23,600 (the maximum ceiling for stipends for clergy of incumbent status), no figures being regionally adjusted.

5.17 The advantages of this model are as follows:

- It affirms the value and importance of parochial ministry by recognizing that the proposed upper end of the incumbents' scale is already used for a number of other posts in the Church such as principals of theological colleges and courses, (where the Lichfield Scale recommends that they are paid at the same level as residentiary canons), diocesan directors of education or training, and residentiary canons.
- The range for incumbent status clergy also encompasses residentiary canons, which would mean that it would no longer be necessary to have a separate differential only for residentiary canons.
- It allows recognition of the range of responsibilities held by clergy – parochial and non-parochial – by allowing a higher range of differentials.
- It seems reasonable compared to other differentials in 'senior' posts (see Chapter 4).
- It allows dioceses a greater measure of discretion to take account of their own local circumstances, so that, for example, in the less expensive parts of the country, a diocese could quite reasonably put no one at the very top end (1.3 of the NMS) and very few clergy even at the ceiling for at least 80% of clergy (1.2 of the NMS).
- It is reasonably straightforward to understand and administer.
- The top of the scale (1.3 of the NMS) is a reasonable mid-point between the NMS and the next level of 1.6 of the NMS for archdeacons.

- It acts as a constraint on wealthier dioceses in high cost areas, as their flexibility to pay higher stipends is proportionately reduced by comparison with poorer dioceses and low cost areas.

5.18 The disadvantages of this model are as follows:

- There is a risk that dioceses will simply pay what they can afford.

- The amount of flexibility to pay higher stipends will vary from diocese to diocese. Dioceses where the cost of living is high will have less flexibility to pay higher stipends, and this may be seen as unfair.

- There will be considerable variations in practice between dioceses in the adjustments they make for regional variations in the cost of living and the extent to which they pay differentials, and this may inhibit clergy mobility.

- Some dioceses may find this arrangement will be too expensive, and it will not include all dioceses.

5.19 The Group was not able to reach a decision about the levels of the ceilings and the regionalization of incumbents' stipends. **We recommend that these issues are taken forward for further discussion within the Church in the hope of achieving a consensus on a national stipends structure.**

chapter 6

the process of setting stipends

the role of the Central Stipends Authority

6.1 Clergy stipends are set by dioceses and the Church Commissioners in the light of recommendations made by the Central Stipends Authority (CSA), which was set up in 1972, when the Church Commissioners were appointed as CSA. The Commissioners' responsibilities and powers as CSA were transferred to the Archbishops' Council, by the Central Stipends Authority Regulation 1998, which requires the CSA to consult dioceses and the Church Commissioners about stipends and to make recommendations about stipend levels. The recommendations from 1 April 2001 are shown at **Appendix 4**.

6.2 The purpose of these recommendations is to provide, in partnership with the dioceses and the Church Commissioners, a framework for a national policy for stipends. The aim is to ensure a reasonable degree of stipends coherence across the whole country, and to reflect the self-understanding of the Church of England as being a national Church, offering a ministry to all. Conformity of stipends between dioceses is also seen as important in promoting clergy mobility throughout the country. This does not, however, mean that there should be either a simplistic equality of stipend levels or that there is no place for local flexibility. It is rather that variations in stipend levels should be placed under reasonable constraint. Dioceses are not required to follow the CSA's recommendations, and the case for dioceses having flexibility to set stipend levels becomes increasingly strong, as parishes fund an increasing proportion of the stipends bill.

6.3 The main principles behind the CSA's recommendations are that stipends should be:

> **adequate** for clergy to discharge their duties without undue financial anxiety;
> **flexible** enough to allow the Church to pay its clergy where they can best be deployed;

equitable, with stipend levels being broadly convergent and not acting as an impediment to clergy mobility.

the current consultation process

6.4   The annual consultation process involves the following stages, although, in practice, the timing varies from year to year.

December

Dioceses are given the following information:

- Comparison of recent stipend increases with RPI, AEI and recent wage settlements;
- A suggested value for the housing element of the remuneration package, and comparisons with the disposable income of various professions;
- Forecasts for RPI and AEI;
- Illustrations of possible increases in the National Stipend Benchmark, the effect of these on the Regional Stipend Benchmarks, and details, prepared by the Pensions Board's actuary, of the implications for pension contributions.

Dioceses are asked to indicate:

- Their stipend increases for the following April (January in some dioceses);
- Their preferred increase in the CSA's recommendations for the April after that (January in some dioceses);
- The (highly provisional) likely increase in their own clergy stipends for that April (January in some dioceses).

March

The results are compiled and sent out to dioceses who are asked to vote by Single Transferable Vote on the preferred options for stipends increases indicated by dioceses.

May

The results of diocesan voting are discussed at the Inter-Diocesan Finance Forum.

The Church Commissioners are formally consulted about stipend levels.

The Deployment, Remuneration and Conditions of Service Committee (DRACSC) considers the discussion at the Inter-Diocesan Finance Forum and makes a recommendation to the Archbishops' Council about the level of the CSA's recommendations.

June

The Council, in its role as CSA, makes a final decision on recommended stipend levels for the following year.

Dioceses and the Church Commissioners set their stipend levels in the light of these recommendations.

6.5 This is an extended and complex process, but it ensures that dioceses are aware of one another's views and the assumptions they have made about stipend levels in their financial plans, and that they have an opportunity to discuss the level of the stipend with one another.

the recommendations of the Central Stipends Authority

6.6 Each year the CSA recommends a National Stipend Benchmark (NSB) for clergy of incumbent status (£16,910 from 1 April 2001). The NSB is intended to provide a general indication of the level at which incumbents should be paid.

6.7 The CSA also recommends a National Minimum Stipend for incumbents. This figure sets the level of stipend below which full-time incumbents and incumbent status clergy should not be paid. This is also the figure on which pensions are based. Further details are provided in Chapter 8.

6.8 Assistant staff (assistant curates, deacons, deaconesses and licensed lay workers) are paid according to a national scale that is also recommended by the CSA. The scale provides for assistant curates and licensed lay workers to receive annual increases in stipends during the first four years of ministry. Additional payments may be made for seniority or responsibility. Details are given in **Appendix 4**.

The assistant staff scale is not adjusted for regional variations in the cost of living, and many dioceses do not adhere to it, either because they make regional adjustments or because they prefer a scale with fewer or more points on it.

6.9 The CSA also recommends to dioceses a stipend for archdeacons (£25,370 for 2001/02), and all but four dioceses pay the CSA's recommended stipend to archdeacons.

regional variations

6.10 The NSB is adjusted to take account of regional variations in the cost of living to produce Regional Stipend Benchmarks for each diocese. The figures are based on the comparative cost of a standard 'basket of goods' in nine different regions. This information is supplied by the Reward Group, an organization specializing in providing remuneration data. Costs relating to housing and travel – which are the major factors affecting these variations – are stripped out, as clergy do not have to travel to work, and their accommodation is provided free of charge. Inevitably, the Regional Stipend Benchmarks are broad brush and cannot deal with regional variations within a diocese. One example is the position of clergy serving in the Channel Islands.

6.11 Regional variations in the cost of living need to be distinguished from regional variations in living *standards*, particularly as the latter tend to vary much more than the former, For example, whilst household incomes and expenditures in the South East are around 10% above the national average, costs are only 2.5% above the national average. This may be one reason why the more affluent areas of the country are more likely to have a perception that the level of the stipend is not adequate.

diocesan flexibility

6.12 The current system recommends that dioceses pay a stipend of not more than 2.5% above or less than 1.5% below their Regional Stipend Benchmark. However, this still allows dioceses to pay differentials for parochial clergy or clergy with diocesan appointments, as this restriction only applies to the Diocesan Basic Stipend, which is defined as the stipend paid to the largest group of incumbents and incumbent status clergy in the Diocese.

6.13 **We believe that this flexibility is important, and recommend that dioceses should be free to decide which clergy (if any) might receive a higher level of stipend, and that the CSA should not offer guidance on the application of differentials within a diocese.**

acceptance of the CSA's recommendations

6.14 There has never been complete acceptance of the CSA's recommendations by dioceses, although, by and large, the great majority have followed them. During the 28-year history of the CSA, it has not always been the same dioceses that have departed from the CSA's recommendations. This reflects the tendency of the CSA to adjust its recommendations in the light of dioceses' views, and of dioceses not to remain outside a system that the majority are following.

6.15 As dioceses are required to fund an ever-increasing proportion of the total stipends bill, the need for the CSA to consult dioceses and ensure that its recommendations are not excessively detailed or prescriptive has never been greater.

6.16 We still consider, however, that it is important to maintain a nationally coherent system although it should allow a reasonable element of diocesan flexibility. We believe that the CSA has an important role to play in this process, and do not consider that change is required to its powers and responsibilities. **We therefore recommend that the CSA should continue to make national recommendations, and carry out its functions of liaising with dioceses, and sharing information.**

6.17 The CSA makes recommendations to the Church Commissioners about the stipends paid to bishops, deans and provosts, and residentiary canons. These recommendations are not regionally adjusted. The Church Commissioners follow these recommendations.

6.18 The CSA also gives general advice, in response to requests from diocesan offices and clergy, on a broad range of matters connected with clergy remuneration, such as parochial expenses, Council Tax and maternity pay. Matters relating to clergy conditions of service and deployment are also dealt with by the Archbishops' Council staff, who report on all of these aspects to the Council's Deployment, Remuneration and Conditions of Service Committee (DRACSC).

clergy involvement in setting stipends

6.19 It is clearly right for clergy to be fully consulted and adequately
represented in any discussions on the setting of stipends. A further
dimension, where parochial clergy are concerned, is that they will be
largely responsible for raising increases in stipend via the parish share
from their parishioners.

6.20 At national level, clergy are represented on the Deployment,
Recommendation and Conditions of Service Committee, the
Archbishops' Council and the Church Commissioners' Bishoprics and
Cathedrals Committee and Board of Governors. In addition, each
diocese sends three representatives (one of whom must be a member
of General Synod) to the Inter-Diocesan Finance Forum. In some
dioceses, the General Synod member is from the House of Clergy,
while other dioceses send a lay representative.

6.21 Clergy also have opportunity to contribute to discussions on the level
of stipend through being represented on the General Synod, as the
CSA is required to have to have due regard for any resolution of the
General Synod.

6.22 Clergy may also be involved in the setting of their stipends at
diocesan level. Under the Diocesan Stipends Fund Measure 1953,
the bishop is required to obtain the consent of the Diocesan Board of
Finance for the application of income of the Diocesan Stipends Fund.
Under the DBF Measure 1925, not less than two thirds of the DBF
must consist of members of the Diocesan Synod and a majority shall
be lay people. This means that clergy are involved by statute in the
fixing of diocesan stipend levels.

6.23 From time to time, concern is expressed about whether clergy should
vote on stipend levels which affect them personally as this could be
seen as putting them in a position of a conflict of interest. Where
there is a specific requirement for clergy to be involved in such
decisions this may override any general legal principle that would
otherwise preclude them from doing so. However, the Legal Advisory
Commission will be holding discussions with the Charity
Commissioners on this point, and it is, therefore, not possible at this
stage to give a definitive statement on the legal implications of clergy
voting on increases in their own stipends. The Group notes and
supports the further work being carried out on the legal implications of
clergy being involved in stipend decisions, and accepts that further
action will probably be required, once the results of the discussions
with the Charity Commissioners are known.

diocesan remuneration policies

6.24 The Group believes that transparency is of the essence when stipends are being set, and that there needs to be as much clarity as possible over which diocesan clergy receive differentials. **We recommend that each diocese should have a Committee with responsibility for setting remuneration policy in that Diocese.** The Committee should have a constitution and a published remuneration policy. A possible model is provided at the end of this chapter.

6.25 **The Group recommends that these Committees should be statutory bodies established by Measure.** It would be open to dioceses to determine whether they wished an existing body such as the Diocesan Board of Finance or the Bishop's Council to act as the Remuneration Committee. Alternatively, the diocese could set up a separate committee. The committee would be chaired by the diocesan bishop or someone appointed by him. The membership would be required to include the Bishop, the Chairman of the House of Clergy, the Chairman of the House of Laity, and the Chairman of the Diocesan Board of Finance. The question of whether these Committees should be simply advisory to the Bishop or be bodies to which the Bishop delegates his powers to set stipends under the Diocesan Stipends Funds Measure 1953 should be the subject of consultation with dioceses and the Synod's legal advisers.

6.26 **We recommend that these remuneration policies would need to cover the following areas:**

- **what allowance the diocese makes for regional variations in the cost of living;**
- **which posts should carry a differential and how much;**
- **whether the differential is given for a defined period and the reason for it;**
- **how the diocese ensures that the ceilings operate for at least 80% and not more than 20% of incumbent status clergy within the diocese (see Chapter 5).**

6.27 In order to ensure that the Diocesan Remuneration Policies would be published and easily available, **we recommend that each Diocesan Remuneration Policy should be published within the diocese following approval by the diocesan synod, and each year in the CSA's annual report to the General Synod.**

6.28 **We recommend that clergy should be represented on these Remuneration Committees, but accept that further investigation will be required into the legal implications.**

Model Diocesan Remuneration Policy
(to be approved by the Diocesan Synod)

Diocese of ....
Remuneration Committee

X is the Remuneration Committee in the Diocese. The Committee advises the Bishop and his Council, and through them the Diocesan Synod, on appropriate levels of remuneration for clergy in the Diocese. In so doing, it takes account of the policy established by the Diocesan Synod, together with recommendations issued from time to time by the Archbishops' Council as Central Stipends Authority.

The members of the Committee are appointed by the Synod after each triennial election, and are ... The Committee is chaired by ...

The CSA's national guidelines for the stipend year ——/—— include flexibility for regional costs of living, and upper limits on any differentials dioceses may wish to pay as follows:

The National Minimum Stipend (for all full-time stipendiary clergy) is £ ...

The Incumbent's Stipend Guideline is £ ...

The figure which may be paid at least 80% of incumbent status clergy in the diocese is £ ...

The figure above which no more than 20% of incumbent status clergy in the diocese should be paid is £ ...

The maximum stipend for parochial and diocesan clergy (excluding archdeacons) is £ ...

The recommended stipend for archdeacons is £ ...

Diocesan policies for the stipend year ——/— are as follows:

The average cost of living is assessed in this diocese as X% of the national average and this is taken into account in the figures below.

The Diocesan Minimum Stipend is £ ...

The Diocesan Minimum Stipend for incumbents is £ ...

The following posts receive the following payments in addition to

the Diocesan Minimum for incumbents ...

The Diocesan maximum is £ ...

The level paid to residentiary canons is £ ...

The level paid to archdeacons is £ ...

Review

This policy is reviewed by the Committee each year, and reported to the Synod. It forms a source document for the annual Diocesan Budget. It is also reported to the Archbishops' Council as Central Stipends Authority, which includes it in its annual report to the General Synod, to enable diocesan comparisons to be made clear.

[Comment: Annexes to the policy might give details of the new national definition of the stipend, the history of policy in the Diocese, and any systems developed for responsibility payments.]

chapter 7
housing

origins

7.1   The origin of the current tied house system for clergy lies in the middle ages when priests were provided ('endowed') with land. This they farmed, or later on, rented out and so derived an income. Many also had their home on the same land. This created the basic 'remuneration package', including an income and a house. To secure it, clergy were given freehold rights in the property for the tenure of their office.

7.2   Incumbents were affected by the Endowments and Glebe Measure 1976, which transferred the ownership of the glebe land held as endowment to the Diocesan Board of Finance. But ownership of the house remained vested in the incumbent of the benefice (often known as 'benefice property'). The incumbent may not part with possession of the house without the consent of the Diocesan Parsonages Board and the bishop. The consent of the Church Commissioners is also required (but is deemed to have been given in certain circumstances). The net proceeds of sale are allocated, at the discretion of the Diocesan Board of Finance, either to the capital account of the diocesan stipends fund or to the diocesan pastoral account, or divided between the two accounts. The primary responsibility for the upkeep and repair of parsonage houses rests with the Diocesan Parsonages Board under the Repair of Benefice Buildings Measure 1972, although the incumbent retains a duty to take proper care of the house.

7.3   Housing for assistant clergy and diocesan clergy who are not of incumbent status is generally vested in the DBF, either as corporate or parochial property. The Team and Group Ministries Measure 1995 introduced special provisions relating to housing occupied by clergy in a team ministry. Usually a team ministry has a benefice-owned parsonage house and one or more houses owned by the diocese. A parsonage house may not be disposed of without the consent of the team member occupying it, and, in the case of a house owned by the DBF, the team member occupying it has the right to be informed about and to express views on any proposal for disposal or alteration.

7.4 See houses are the property of the Church Commissioners, who are also responsible for their upkeep. Cathedral property is vested in the cathedral corporate body established by section 9 of the Cathedrals Measure 1999. Before disposing of a house occupied by a dean or residentiary canon, the Chapter must obtain that person's consent.

previous work

7.5 The Clergy Conditions of Service Steering Group initiated a wide consultation in 1994. This was published in GS 1173 in November 1995 and debated that month by the General Synod. Provisional conclusion 4 of GS 1173 was that the response to the consultation provided no basis for a fundamental change in the practice of an incumbent living in a house 'provided in his or her benefice'. However, it said that the basis on which property is held should be further examined bearing in mind the need to provide secure houses and that it would be ready to bring forward proposals for reform.

7.6 In 1998, the Diocesan Consultative Group of Chairmen and Secretaries, the Diocesan Finance Forum and the Clergy Conditions of Service Steering Group accepted a joint staff working party's recommendation (after full diocesan consultation) that there was no compelling reason to legislate for a change in the freehold ownership of benefice property (and parsonage houses in particular). The evidence gathered showed that there were only a few cases where the incumbent had prevented the replacement of an unsuitable parsonage house. A review of the Repair of Benefice Buildings Measure 1972 was put in hand. Again, there has been full diocesan consultation and this review is nearing completion.

7.7 The Review Group, however, has a range of comments to make upon the nature and status of provided housing. We note that the issue of principle in respect of the ownership of benefice housing is significantly wider than the questions relating to the replacement of unsuitable parsonage houses. We note that in chapter 18 of its report, *Resourcing Bishops*, the Archbishops' Review Group on Bishops' needs and resources considers the possibility of a transfer of ownership of see houses from the Church Commissioners to the Diocesan Boards of Finance. The Group thus believes that the issue of principle in respect of the ownership of the benefice house remains open to further review and investigation; hence the recommendation formulated in paragraph 7.31.

the nature of the tied house system

7.8   In our consultation, we received many comments on the existing tied house system. These ranged from the view that the tied house was 'a form of slavery' and 'fostered a dependency culture among clergy', to those who are entirely happy with the tied house system and would want dioceses to take on more responsibilities.

7.9   The possibility of clergy providing their own houses, with a compensating adjustment to the stipend, has been considered by the Review Group. This is a pattern which is seen in some other provinces of the Anglican Communion (for example, in the USA). It is however noteworthy that the taxation system for housing in the USA differs from that in the UK and is considerably more generous to home owners. A sizeable minority of clergy in ECUSA live in church-provided housing – interestingly, more in the east where the patterns are inherited from the early settlers from Europe. Other Anglican provinces we looked at generally provided housing.

7.10   Different arrangements apply in other Churches. For example, we were made aware of the practices of the Church in Denmark and the Church of Sweden. In both these churches, clergy housing is owned by the parish and is rented to clergy occupiers at a rent which may well approach a commercial level. In both these Baltic churches, the Church is a State church and partly or fully financed by a church tax. The history of all the examples we have looked at, as with the Church of England, is for the clergy to be provided with housing.

the wishes of clergy

7.11   The Group was made well aware that many clergy want to be able to buy their own homes, enabling them to have the accommodation that is suitable for their family and other needs. It would also enable the clergy to build up equity in property towards the time when they will retire and have to provide their own housing. This was clearly an area that we wished to pursue but we noted that the issue relates more to the ability of clergy to build up some capital/equity in property for their retirement, than to their wish to get involved in the housing market during their active ministry. We noted that around 30% of clergy reaching retirement participate in the CHARM Scheme (Church's Housing Assistance to the Retired Ministry), and so presumably have little or no capital. This proportion may well decline, as ordinands have not been required to sell any house they owned to fund training since 1990.

the advantages and disadvantages of the tied house

7.12 We looked at this from several viewpoints. It is first worth summarizing the main advantages and disadvantages of the tied house system. This table sets out the main factors with no attempt to balance them.

Advantages	Disadvantages
Long history	No unfettered choice in where to live
Eases mobility and deployment	Expectation of constant availability
Provides a local pastoral base	Home is also place of work for meetings and callers – there is a lack of privacy, both perceived and actual
Tax benefits	No equity in housing for retirement
Protects clergy stipends from house inflation	Occasional lack of 'tenant upkeep' as this is seen as the responsibility of the diocese
Centralized funding and management, economies of scale	Housing provided in Urban Priority Areas is not typical of the area
	Bills for services are greater than if clergy were simply housing themselves

tax benefits

7.13 Although the majority of clergy are not employees, they are treated for purposes of tax and national insurance as if they were. There are two areas of particular note in the taxation of the clergy. First, by virtue of the requirement to live in the provided house, the clergy are deemed to be in 'representative occupation' whereby such accommodation is provided for the better performance of duties. Therefore, no tax charge is levied on the provision of the house, as would be the case, for example, if a company provided a house for a director. Second, a proportion of the stipend may be paid free of tax and national insurance in respect of reimbursement of the cost of heating, lighting and cleaning of the official house. This benefit, however, is restricted by the operation of a clawback mechanism known as 'service benefit' and the result is thus a modest tax benefit to the clergy.

7.14   However two important facts should be noted. Firstly, the tax situation serves the Church well not only in respect of the basic provision of the house but also in respect of some other housing costs, for example, Council Tax and water rates. If these costs were taken on by the clergy occupiers, they would have to come from taxed income, which would be more expensive than the current situation. Secondly those clergy employed by organizations such as theological colleges and courses that base their stipends on that of incumbents of the Church of England, are less well off than incumbents due to the favourable tax treatment of the latter. The heating, lighting and cleaning allowance is only of value to those in an official house and undertaking full-time duties, although the Inland Revenue may give a study allowance in other circumstances. It must be up to the bodies concerned to decide how they set their stipends, but we offer this as a 'health warning' to them.

the provided house as a pastoral tool

7.15   There are many parishes up and down the country where the 'Vicarage' is the centre of parish activities – a meeting place, the place where the church fete is held each year, a place of calm and care. In many cases, it would not be practicable for a prospective incumbent to purchase a house which provided such facilities. In some areas there would simply not be a house (even of a lower standard) that could be afforded, while in others no privately owned housing is available. This would have severe effects on the national deployability of clergy that is so vital a feature of the Church of England. Thus if all our clergy houses were sold, it would be extremely difficult to secure local pastoral care and the Church of England would see many of its clergy commuting a considerable distance between their home and the parish. It would lead to the loss of the traditional pattern of clergy living and working among their parishioners, and although this is the pattern in some parts of the USA, the expectations of the clergy there are very different from those in the Church of England. Commuting costs would have to be paid out of taxed income and clergy would have to buy and sell houses at regular intervals. As one priest said, 'An incumbent changing benefices has quite enough on his plate without having added to it the problem of finding himself a house to live in.'

7.16   Although provided accommodation is undoubtedly a benefit, the particular drawbacks need to be acknowledged.

   i)   Clergy are generally required by virtue of their office to live in the accommodation provided and thus have no unfettered choice in where they live.

ii) Clergy generally want to be available at home/office to their parishioners, and, even if clergy take appropriate time off, and use devices such as answerphones, there is an expectation in many minds of constant availability.

iii) Part of the accommodation is office space and is frequently used for meetings and offering hospitality. The tax allowance for heating, lighting and cleaning reflects this usage.

iv) Clergy have to provide accommodation for themselves and their families on retirement. (The formula for calculating the pension and retirement lump sum makes allowance for this fact.)

the cost to the Church and the clergy

7.17 We looked at the cost to the Church of a change to owner occupation. It is only possible to make some broad assumptions here, but we believe them to be reasonable.

7.18 What savings would be made? It is to be expected that the cost to a typical diocesan budget of the housing elements of the remuneration package would be reasonably similar to the relevant figures set out in Chapter 3 for a detached house. The figures only differ markedly if one includes in the calculations an element for the income foregone on the capital value tied up in the housing. If one assumes an average value of £175,000 and an average real income (after allowing for inflation) of 2.5%, the 'cost' to the Church of providing the capital in tied accommodation is about £4,375 per year per house. Looked at the other way round, this is also the annual amount of real income that would be available if the house were sold and the proceeds invested.

7.19 If the Church sold its houses and paid extra stipend, it would cost the Church (as seen above, and including the tax advantages of the current situation) about £12,570 p.a. in extra stipend to allow the provision of housing to a standard similar to that now existing. Towards this, the Church would have £4,375 p.a. from the capital arising from sale proceeds, and some £2,000 a year from savings on outgoings. There is therefore a net cost to the Church in moving to owner occupation of some £6,195 p.a. per house. To provide a stipend level sufficient to pay for a house of the current standards would cost the Church significantly more. We think it unlikely that this would attract the Church at large.

7.20 If clergy were to become owner occupiers, they would have less time for pastoral duties (or their families for other activities). At present they are relieved of the time cost of all the routine maintenance tasks that occupy so much of the 'spare' time of the typical house-owner. This is done for them by the staff of the diocese, or the parish officers. There is none of the time or financial pressure associated with mortgage rate changes, rent rises, Council Tax rises, etc. At its best, the diocese provides a 'one-stop shop' housing service that is unfortunately often hidden from the view of many parishioners and less appreciated than it should be. The expert advice of a professional surveyor is not available to most house-owners, who either have to pay for it, or go without. Many dioceses ensure that housing systems come with procedures for occupiers that rival the best in the rented sector, and if all else fails, the archdeacon can come along to sort it out! These provisions would be lost in a change to owner occupation – we do not believe that would be welcomed by most clergy.

7.21 At present, the tied house provides space for an office, study, meetings and hospitality. To change this would mean an extra cost in many parishes. Although the Green Guide urges that new houses should be homes for clergy and their families, and not administrative centres for the parishes, it is clear that in many cases, there is no alternative, or this is what the parish or priest is used to. To make a change would deeply affect the work of parishes – we do not believe this would attract most parishes or clergy.

conclusions on the tied house

7.22 The Group concluded that there are considerable pastoral advantages to the Church of England in maintaining a policy of providing housing for its stipendiary clergy. This makes a clear statement about the commitment of the Church in every local community, despite the ability to change properties from time to time as pastoral and other needs dictate.

7.23 **It is the Group's clear recommendation that the Church of England does not change from its existing position of providing housing for clergy as part of their remuneration package.**

future improvements

7.24 The Group also considered that there are several areas where it is considered that the existing system could be improved.

provision for retirement

7.25   The Group considered evidence concerning the inability of the clergy to accumulate capital through the acquisition of freehold property over the course of their working lives. Although the evidence is somewhat distorted by the phenomenon of significant levels of capital appreciation in recent years, and also by the fact that there are notable regional variations, the Group recognizes that the ability to purchase a property on a mortgage and rent it out is likely to lead to advantages denied to clergy who do not have access to the housing market. This will be especially the case when there is inflation. We note from the survey that around 40% of clergy either own or are purchasing a property on a mortgage. The concern therefore for the other 60% of clergy is how to encourage early access to the housing market so that provision for retirement housing can be made over the course of a minister's career which might enable other advantages to accrue. The low level of clergy stipends is a barrier to entry to the market. This matter is further discussed in chapter 8.

clarity and communication

7.26   Whilst the Church Commissioners have the responsibility for setting national guidelines for the provision of houses for incumbents, it is up to each diocese to develop its policies in relation to its existing housing stock. It is also for each diocese, and perhaps, where appropriate, parishes, to determine the appropriate policies in respect of assistant staff housing. The same could be true of archdeacons and bishops where dioceses and the Church Commissioners have separate policies. The Group was made aware that a number of dioceses have clear policy guidelines relating to the standards of accommodation and the mutual expectations of the clergy and the diocese in respect of any work to be done to the house. Such policies are often set out in a residents' or occupiers' guide. We consider that much is to be gained by setting out very clearly what the mutual expectations of the 'employer' and 'employee' are in respect of the housing element of the remuneration package. There is ample room for bad feeling and criticism on both sides if these matters are not set out clearly. **Accordingly, we recommend that every diocese should have such policies in place, have them approved by their Diocesan Synod or other appropriate body, and communicate them widely to the clergy and parishes.**

7.27 In a similar way, many dioceses have developed polices in respect of the standards of assistant staff accommodation. **Again, we recommend that these should be published widely so that there is clarity between all parties involved.**

occupation costs

7.28 At present, dioceses provide accommodation free of rent, Council Tax, water charges and all repairs and improvements. The clergy are expected to pay the normal outgoings from the house including gas, electricity and telephone. It has been put to us that a change should be made in respect of water charges. These were originally levied on the basis of the rateable value of houses and, like the formal domestic rates, were paid by the diocese. There is an increasing trend for water companies to impose a requirement for water meters in new houses, and to encourage occupiers to move to metered water supplies. Depending on the number of members of the family, the water consumption will differ in such circumstances and therefore the cost to the diocese will vary accordingly. Whilst many clergy would wish to follow the encouragement of the water company and save water, they have no financial incentive to do so as any savings are made by the diocese. In these circumstances, it is argued that water charges should be borne by the occupier of the houses as they increasingly relate to the consumption through the property. It also appears that a similar situation exists in respect of the Council Tax, which is partially related to the number of occupiers, although primarily on capital value.

7.29 However, the tax implications of such a change to the Church, as described above, strongly argue against such change. Clearly there would also have to be an adjustment to the stipend if this change was made. **Although there is much to be gained in terms of clarity and accountability for clergy to bear the cost of water charges, we recommend that no further work to pursue this be undertaken.**

7.30 Some dioceses already delegate responsibility for payment of water charges, Council Tax, and some other minor costs connected with houses, to parishes and occupiers. It is obviously desirable for the cost of these elements of the remuneration package to be clearly communicated in order to show parishes the true cost of having a priest. It is up to dioceses to arrange such delegation as they think fit but it does appear to be expedient for such schemes to be clarified, and eventually distinctions minimized, when dioceses discuss levels of stipend.

legal arrangements

7.31 The Group considered that the complex legal arrangements relating to the ownership of the different categories of clergy housing are the result of a lack of coherence in such matters in the past. There are no less than seven different categories of ownership managed by four different bodies. These have arisen by accident of history and appear to cause confusion in the minds of church people and the wider public alike. There are also additional administrative costs connected with this complex web of arrangements. The Group did not consider that making a recommendation to clarify this complexity was within its terms of reference. It was also put to the Group that some clergy would strongly oppose any change in the ownership of the house which they would see as an infringement of the freehold. The Group did not itself consider that a simplification of the legal arrangements of Church housing need pose any threat at all to the freehold of office. **Accordingly, we recommend that further work to simplify the Church's legal systems be undertaken at an early date by dioceses, the Archbishops' Council and Church Commissioners.**

7.32 The Group is aware that, by basically recommending the continuation of the status quo in respect of clergy housing, it will not please those who have strongly advocated change. The Group sympathizes with such views although, on the balance of the evidence before it, it was clear to us that the financial, historical, sociological, pastoral and ecclesiological arguments are all in favour of retaining, but seeking to improve the existing system.

chapter 8
pensions

the present provisions of the scheme

8.1 The Rules of most occupational pension schemes define a 'normal retirement age'. This is a pivotal factor and it usually corresponds to the contractual age of retirement in the employment that gives rise to membership of the scheme. As the majority of clergy are not employed, there is no contractual age of retirement. The Ecclesiastical Offices (Age Limit) Measure 1975 fixed a maximum age of 70 for vacating an office and this now applies to all but a very small number of those in office. The Pensions Measures have thus always set what is, in effect, a 'minimum normal pension age'. At one time it was 70, but it was reduced in stages and the legislation was formally changed to make it 65 with effect from 6 April 1978.

8.2 The qualifying period of pensionable service for the full rate of pension, on retirement at or after the minimum pension age, was at one time 40 years. It was reduced to 37 years when the minimum pension age was lowered. For those who have completed a shorter period of service, the calculation of the pension (and lump sum) is directly proportionate. Those who remain in office after age 65 continue to accrue additional pension rights (until their pensionable service reaches 37 years).

8.3 Retirement before age 65 with an immediate pension and lump sum used to be possible only if an individual was in ill-health. A provision for voluntary early retirement was introduced in 1988. The calculation of the pension and lump sum under the latter follows the principle of offering immediate benefits that have equal value to the prospective entitlement at age 65 in respect of the period of pensionable service performed. For those awarded a disability pension after consideration of the medical report submitted, the calculation takes into account prospective service to age 65 and there is no reduction for early payment.

8.4 Also in 1988, a lump sum death benefit – previously arranged separately – was included in the scheme. This is three times pensionable stipend where death occurs in service under the age of 65.

8.5 The main elements of the benefits provided by the pension scheme were agreed by the General Synod in 1980, following discussion of a detailed report *The Pensions of the Full-time Ministry* (GS 464) from the Pensions Board and the Church Commissioners. They are:

Full service pension, on retirement at or after age 65	Two-thirds of the National Minimum Stipend in the previous year
Retirement lump sum	Three times the pension
Widow(er)'s pension	Two-thirds of scheme member's prospective pension

8.6 These targets were attained in stages, the first being reached in 1985 with full implementation in 1990. The current figures are:

National Minimum Stipend at 1.4.00	£15,570
Full service pension from 1.4.01	£10,380
Retirement lump sum	£31,140
Widow(er)'s pension	£6,920
Lump sum on death in full-time pensionable service before age 65	£46,710

8.7 The validity of the benefit bases was retested in 1991 (*The Pension Scheme for those in the Stipendiary Ministry*, GS 987) after the targets agreed in 1980 had all been fully attained. The bases were reviewed again in a further detailed paper (*Pensions for those in the Stipendiary Ministry: The Calculation of Benefits for Future Service and the Contributions Required*, GS 1208) by the Pensions Board, following the decision to establish a separately funded pension scheme in respect of future service. The circumstances which had led to that radical change in the financial arrangements caused great uncertainty among those in the stipendiary ministry. Affirmation by the Synod of the basis for calculating retirement benefits, without change, together with a smooth transition to the new arrangements allayed those concerns.

8.8 The benefits resulting from pensionable service up to 31 December 1997 are set out in the Church of England Pensions Regulations. Benefits arising from service on or after 1 January 1998 are set out in the Trust Deed and Rules of the Funded Scheme.

concept of pensions as deferred pay

8.9 'Defined Benefits' (also known as 'Final Salary') occupational pension schemes – that is those which base benefits at retirement on years of pensionable service and salary close to retirement – generally incorporate the individual's own salary in that calculation. A principle of the clergy scheme is that all (full-time) service that is pensionable is to be treated equally. Thus a national stipend indicator is used throughout, rather than individual stipends.

8.10 Most of those covered either remain in pensionable service under the scheme until retirement or return after a period outside its scope. The scheme is operated on a national basis so those moving from one diocese (or other participating body) to another are not treated as leavers and new entrants. Similarly, all periods of pensionable service are aggregated at retirement and benefits calculated in respect of the total at the level then applicable. A major disadvantage of 'defined benefits' schemes for early leavers thus does not apply. The concept of an occupational pension being part of 'remuneration' in the form of 'deferred pay' is straightforward and widely accepted. The bases for calculating the benefits provided by the clergy pension scheme reflect best practice, but they contain a number of distinctive characteristics as does their derivation.

8.11 A stipend has been considered to be a 'living allowance', not a reward for services, and the National Minimum Stipend was defined as just adequate for that purpose, so long as housing was provided and expenses of office were reimbursed. The National Minimum Stipend was thus used as the starting point for deriving a pension formula. Account was then taken of cessation of the liability to pay National Insurance contributions and receipt of a state pension in retirement, but also the change at retirement in responsibility for meeting the cost of housing. Finally, allowance was made for part of the benefits 'package' being given in the form of a lump sum.

link between pensions and stipends

8.12 It was mentioned in paragraph 8.9 that 'defined benefits' schemes generally reflect salary close to retirement in determining the benefits payable at that point. In relating the result of the arithmetical exercise, described in paragraph 8.11, back to the stipend, however, a convenient formula was obtained by the use of the previous year's National Minimum Stipend. When stipend increases are relatively stable, there is no resulting difficulty. Although in the longer term the pension follows the stipend, the year-by-year changes will be out of step when the rate of stipend increase is rising or falling markedly.

8.13 The much lower present level of inflation, and hence of stipend increases compared with when the formula was derived in 1980, means that the pension is now a higher proportion of current stipend. The state pension, which is an important part of clergy income after retirement, has however declined relative to earnings and to the stipend, while housing costs have risen in relative terms. The overall effect is that the present pension figure is nearly £1,000 lower than would arise from application of the arithmetical process adopted in establishing the current benefit formula (described in paragraph 8.9). The gap has narrowed a little this year compared with last year, as a result of the larger than usual rise in the state pension.

increases to pensions in payment

8.14 It has been a statutory requirement since 1997 that 'defined benefits' schemes increase the pension after retirement to reflect 'Limited Price Indexation' (LPI) – that is the rise in the Retail Prices Index but with an upper limit of 5% in any one year. Most schemes of this kind give increases which have regard to that obligation or, at best, fully match price inflation.

8.15 The declared aim for the clergy scheme, last reaffirmed by the General Synod in 1996, is to increase the pension after retirement in line with the annual increase in the stipend. This ensures that all clergy who retire at or after the pension age and who have served 37 or more years are entitled to the same level of pension, regardless of the date of their retirement. This provision formed an integral part of a retirement package related to a stipend which is deemed to be 'a living allowance'.

8.16 The scheme documentation provides for increases in line with LPI and for higher increases at the discretion of the Church Commissioners (in respect of pensions arising from pre-1998 service) or the Pensions Board (in respect of pensions from service after 1997). The contribution rate under the funded scheme makes allowance for that discretion to be exercised, having regard to the intention agreed by the General Synod.

matters for discussion

8.17 The Group noted that, if stipend levels are no better than adequate, the current quantum of pension is not over generous either in relation to stipends or in absolute terms. It felt, however, that a number of details of the provisions of the pension scheme were in need of reconsideration.

8.18 The derivation of the existing pension formula was based on a number of principles:

- a stipend is a living allowance;
- the National Minimum Stipend is 'just adequate' for that purpose
- there is a national stipends structure;
- the Church supports a uniform national pension scheme;
- housing (or an allowance) is provided in addition to the stipend.

Whilst three of the above would remain, the Group has decided to recommend a change in the concept of the stipend (Chapter 2) and that 'adequacy' should no longer feature in the definition of the stipend.

8.19 As a consequence of these changes, the Group was minded to propose that the provisions of the Scheme should be more in line with those of occupational pension schemes generally. We set out in the following paragraphs the areas in which amendments might be made. We did not complete our deliberations, however, as a result of the news in April 2001 of the increase in the contribution rate for the existing benefit structure disclosed by the triennial actuarial valuation. This led to the establishment by The Archbishops' Council of the Financial Issues Working Group, to which several members of the Review Group and all its assessors belong.

period of accrual to qualify for full pension on retirement at the pension age

8.20 We noted that this would typically be 40 years. The maximum period from ordination to pension age is 42 years. The existing basis under the scheme – 37 years – took into account, *inter alia*, the mix of actual ordination ages and the limited benefits retained by early leavers from previous employment. Changes resulting from primary legislation have meant that the latter point is of reduced significance today.

stipend to which pension calculation is related

8.21 We noted that National Minimum Stipend in the previous year was adopted to fit the original arithmetic. Since there is a possibility of difficulties arising in the event of changing economic conditions, we would be inclined to use the current, rather than previous year's figure.

The choice would lie between the NMS and Incumbent's Stipend Guideline. The one selected would not necessarily affect the resulting quantum of pension as the calculation formula would be pitched accordingly.

service after age 65

8.22 At present such service only adds to the accrual of benefits until an overall total of 37 years pensionable service has been achieved. This approach reflects, *inter alia*, the flexibility of actual retirement date open to the individual. It is consistent with ending accrual for those under age 65 once 37 years have been completed. We have looked at an alternative approach, whereby accrual prior to age 65 is limited to the selected 'full service' period, but service after age 65 (up to a maximum of 5 years) accrues additional benefits. This would offer an incentive to those contemplating staying in post, even if they had already completed the basic period of full service. A further, related, consideration would be setting the statutory *retirement* age at 65, so that continuation would need the agreement of the diocesan bishop.

increases to pensions in payment

8.23 The current approach, and the statutory requirement, are both set out in paragraphs 8.1 – 8.16. It would be consistent with bringing the provisions of the clergy scheme into line with occupational schemes generally if the changes made included raising pensions, after they come into payment, to reflect LPI rather than stipend increases. There would, however, continue to be a discretionary power which would enable higher increases to be given, if they could be afforded, were price inflation to exceed 5% in any year.

application of a revised structure

8.24 We have received clear legal advice that changes to the documented provisions of the pension scheme could only be applied in respect of pensionable service after a future date. The position in respect of determining the level of increases to pensions once in payment is less certain. Whilst only LPI is documented, the General Synod has nevertheless affirmed on a number of occasions a commitment to increases in line with the rate of rise in stipends. It might well thus be felt that a change should apply only as part of a revised package for future service.

8.25 It could be argued that the revised provisions of the Scheme should only apply to new entrants after the specified future date, with existing members continuing on the current bases for the remainder of their pensionable service. Alternatively it might be thought that the revisions should apply to all *service* after that date, since the new stipends structure would apply to all.

costs

8.26 We recognize that the costs of a pension scheme cannot be known until they are actually incurred. Nevertheless, we feel that indicated rates of contribution give a reasonable comparison of the potential costs of different benefit structures.

8.27 We had begun to look at two possible models for a revised scheme. Whilst these would have produced a 'full service' pension similar in amount to that under the existing arrangements, they incorporated changes in detail which have been referred to in the section 'Matters for Discussion' (paragraphs 8.17ff.). The effect of a lower accrual rate per year of service (and consequent smaller proportion of members achieving the full pension) together with the change to the calculation of post-retirement increases would be to reduce the contributions indicated compared with those for the existing benefit structure.

members' contributions

8.28 A suggestion that clergy and the other members of the scheme should pay contributions was considered in 1996 when the Funded Scheme was in the process of being established. The General Synod accepted that it would not be reasonable to require members to start to contribute without a commensurate increase in stipends.

8.29 Although there would be no resulting change to an individual's tax liability, as relief would be available on the contributions, the additional stipend would attract increases in both 'employee's' and 'employer's' National Insurance contributions. Neutralizing the individual's financial position would have resulted in an overall annual additional cost to the Church of £1.25 million. Recording members' contributions would also have increased the cost of scheme administration. The Synod agreed that any perceived presentational advantage of contributions by members was outweighed by the financial cost to the Church.

8.30 The position has not changed since 1996. The amount of the additional cost would, however, now be higher.

a more radical change

8.31 As mentioned in paragraph 8.9, the existing scheme is what is known as a 'Final Salary' or 'Defined Benefits' one. Under this type of scheme, the documentation sets out calculation bases which link the benefits payable in various circumstances to salary. Generally this will be the individual member's salary, but the use of a uniform stipend does not affect the concept. There is an underlying commitment by the employer to meet the costs of providing the benefits calculated on the specified bases. Benefits are fixed, but the costs are variable.

8.32 The other main type of scheme is 'Money Purchase' or 'Defined Contributions'. Under such schemes, the employer is committed to paying a certain level of contributions and the benefits received by the member reflect the accumulation of the contributions paid. Costs are fixed, but the benefits are variable.

8.33 The contribution rate for a defined benefit scheme is, for convenience, usually expressed as a percentage of the total pensionable payroll. This does not mean, however, that the employer is paying that percentage in respect of each individual member. The cost is much lower for a younger member than for an older one. Application of a uniform percentage under a defined contribution scheme would thus be too generous for young members and decidedly inadequate for older ones. A way to offset this problem would be to have a scale of contribution rates (in age bands). This does, however, reduce the clarity of the employer's overall costs, while adding to the complexity both of administration and for members.

8.34 The key difference between the 'Defined Benefit' and 'Defined Contributions' approaches is the location of risk. Under the former it lies with the employer, whereas under the latter it lies with the member.

8.35 At an early stage in our deliberations we looked at these alternative approaches to pension provision. Before the Group had finally agreed its recommendations, the outcome of the actuarial review of the pension fund was announced. This was quickly followed by the setting up by the Archbishops' Council of a group to review certain financial issues, including future pension arrangements as mentioned in paragraph 8.19. **The Group recommends that the issues discussed in paragraph 8.17ff. are taken forward by this and any subsequent group.**

differentials

8.36 The usual understanding of pensions is to see them as deferred pay. If we are correct in holding that differentials in stipend are theologically, ethically and practically just, then the same principle can be applied to pensions. However it should be noted that the current pension differentials are substantially less than the current stipend differentials. The basic pension is payable in full to all clergy who have completed 37 years service. Differentials thereafter are:

Retired suffragan bishops, deans, provosts and archdeacons	1.25 times the basic pension
Retired diocesan bishops	1.5 times the basic pension
Retired bishops of London	1.8 times the basic pension
Retired archbishops	2 times the basic pension

There is no differential in the lump sum payable. With the addition of the state pension the differentials in total income would be further lessened.

8.37 While we believe the basic arguments for differentials in stipend justify these pension differentials there is one further practical argument for retaining them. Under current legislation if institutions are to be allowed to opt out of SERPS (the State Earnings Related Pensions Scheme) pensions must be related in some way to final earnings. The current levels of pensions differentials allow such opting out. If the differentials were further lessened it would make such opting out very difficult.

8.38 **Accordingly we recommend that there should be no changes in the current pension differentials.**

retirement housing

8.39 Clergy in office are paid a stipend and are provided with housing (or a housing allowance). They do not have to meet from their stipend either the capital cost of accommodation or a number of running costs – maintenance, buildings insurance, water rates – nor the Council Tax. They do, however, have to meet these costs in relation to retirement housing. As was explained in paragraph 8.11, account was taken of this in deriving the formula for determining retirement benefits under the pension scheme.

8.40   A long-standing facility under which the Pensions Board assists clergy to obtain retirement housing, if they have insufficient resources of their own for this purpose, was also reviewed in the early 1980s. The facility is also available to widow(er)s of clergy. The principles of the current scheme were agreed by the Synod in 1982 after consideration of a joint report *The Church's Housing Assistance for the Retired Ministry* (GS 540) from the Board and the Church Commissioners. Since 1983 the Board's own resources have been substantially extended through capital loans from the Commissioners on terms that include linking the value of a loan to the value of the property. The Commissioners also provide financial support of the revenue costs under the housing scheme. The 1996 paper about the pension scheme (GS 1208) affirmed the continuing need for the housing facility.

8.41   A continuation of the provision by the Church of housing for those in office would mean that those retiring would still need to switch, on retirement, to housing arranged (and financed) by themselves. Although many do this without recourse to the scheme through the Pensions Board, a significant number do make use of it.

8.42   There are a number of parameters – regarding size of property and price (although the latter varies to reflect market conditions in different areas) – within which the Board operates that scheme. The underlying reason for these restrictions is that the capital available for the scheme cannot be unlimited. It is necessary, therefore, to attempt to ensure that assistance will be available to those with the most need. We understand, however, that the Board is currently reviewing the operational parameters to see if some measure of greater flexibility would be possible.

8.43   Another perceived disadvantage of the scheme is that mortgages can only be obtained from the Board up to three years before the pension age (or on earlier retirement) and a Board-owned property can only be arranged during the months immediately prior to retirement. The clergy survey revealed that 38% of clergy do own a residential property. We believe that many others would welcome the opportunity to do so, but do not have any capital to use as a deposit while obtaining a loan in the conventional mortgage market.

8.44 In our view, were they in a position to do so, they would be able to cover the costs of the finance and outgoings on the property by letting it until they were approaching retirement. **Accordingly, we recommend that the Pensions Board, the Church Commissioners, dioceses and other possible sources of funding consider the possibility of finding sufficient capital for loans to provide the 'pump priming' for this purpose.**

chapter 9
other issues

clergy expenses

9.1 The recommendations of the Central Stipends Authority (CSA) are made on the basis that all clergy expenses are fully reimbursed. This means that clergy whose expenses are not fully reimbursed are not receiving their full stipend.

9.2 The CSA makes efforts to encourage the full reimbursement of expenses in the following ways:

- By publishing the levels at which expenses are reimbursed in each diocese in its annual report to the General Synod;

- By promoting the full reimbursement of expenses by means of its booklet *The Parochial Expenses of the Clergy*. This is regularly updated, and is available free of charge on request to the Central Stipends Authority.

9.3 Results from the survey of clergy indicate the following:

- Two-thirds (66%) of respondents had expenses between £1,000 and £5,000.

- One-sixth (15%) of respondents voluntarily chose not to claim expenses. The amounts varied from under £1,000 to above £5,000.

- One-sixth (16%) of respondents did not feel able to claim some of their expenses. In the majority of cases, these were for amounts below £1,000, but there were 222 clergy unable to claim amounts of £1,000 – £2,000, 114 unable to claim for amounts of £2,000 – £5,000 and 8 who did not feel able to claim for amounts over £5,000.

9.4 Returns from clergy indicate that the extent of unreimbursed expenses continues very slowly to fall. For the stipends year 2000/01 the average amount of expenses unreimbursed was £160, representing 9.1% of average total expenses of £1,750. This is encouraging as an overall trend, particularly at a time when parishes are having to assume an ever-larger proportion of the costs of pensions and stipends. However, despite this progress, the level of failure to reimburse expenses is unacceptably high, especially if the possibility of under-reporting of expenses and occasional pressures not to claim are taken into account.

the taxation of clergy

9.5 Clergy do not have to pay tax on their accommodation, which is usually provided rent-free. Nor do they have to pay tax on amounts paid towards the maintenance of their housing such as external decoration, insurance or water charges. They are not liable for Council Tax on their provided accommodation.

9.6 Under arrangements agreed with the Inland Revenue, a proportion of the stipend may be paid tax-free in reimbursement of heating, lighting, cleaning and garden upkeep costs (known as HLC), provided that clergy occupy an official house provided for duties which are full time. They are required, however, to pay tax (known as 'service benefit') on this arrangement, and the main value to clergy is that they do not pay National Insurance on the HLC.

9.7 Clergy in receipt of a stipend and no other income, depending on their family and financial circumstances, are likely to be eligible to receive Working Families Tax Credit, as the Inland Revenue takes a generous view of the value of provided accommodation when assessing the amount of tax credits that clergy are eligible to receive. The survey of clergy suggested that about one-twentieth (5%) of respondents (just over 300 clergy) had received or were about to claim Working Families Tax Credit.

9.8 It seems unlikely that a change to the concept of the stipend from living allowance to the rate for the job would affect the taxation of the clergy, as, for tax purposes, stipend is regarded as income or emoluments from office.

job security and employment rights

9.9 Many clergy have the protection of the freehold, which provides a higher level of job security than that of employees. Job security has often been used to justify lower remuneration (for example in the Civil Service). However, it is very difficult to put a precise figure on the value of such security.

9.10 More significantly, some clergy (mainly priests-in-charge and assistant curates) and licensed lay workers do not have the freehold and are less secure than employees. Work is being carried out on ways in which their job security might be improved.

9.11 The Government has taken powers under the Employment Relations Act 1999 to confer on ministers of religion some of the rights of employees. Its consultation paper has yet to be published, but the Church has set up a group to look at ways of ensuring that, whatever the details of the Government's proposals, the Church moves towards best practice in these areas.

9.12 If clergy were to acquire the rights of employees as set out in the Employment Relations Act 1999, this would be unlikely to affect the tax position of clergy.

additional earnings

9.13 Under the current arrangements, the level of stipend is adjusted to take account of unassigned parochial fees, additional earnings from chaplaincies and part-time appointments. As a result, clergy of incumbent status should receive the same total income, whether or not they are paid for chaplaincies and part-time appointments.

9.14 These arrangement came into effect in 1975, when the General Synod approved the *Method of Computing Income for Augmentation Purposes*, which is reproduced each year as an annex to the annual report of the Central Stipends Authority. As a result there is now broad consistency throughout the whole Church in the treatment of additional payments made to clergy. Details are given in **Appendix 6**.

9.15 Although the Method of Computing Income requires the level of stipend to be adjusted to take account of income from chaplaincies (net of any unreimbursed expenses), it allows clergy to retain income from earnings relating to work done during their spare time. What 'spare-time earnings' means needs to be determined in the light of the actual circumstances of each individual case, but the guidance offered by the CSA suggests that work could be regarded as spare time if the following factors applied:

   i) The work can be carried out in time that would not otherwise be devoted to parochial duties.

   ii) The work can continue in the event of a move to another parish.

iii) The work can be undertaken at a time and place of the clergyperson's choosing.

iv) The work does not require absence from the parish exceeding the recommended period of annual leave.

9.16 The Group does not consider that further direction is desirable in this area. Where any additional work adversely affects the performance of parochial duties, this will potentially be a discipline matter. **The Group therefore recommends that the General Synod's Method of Computing Income should be retained.**

payments to clergy from charitable sources by dioceses and charities

9.17 The Group wrote to diocesan bishops and clergy charities, asking them for details of the assistance they provided to clergy.

9.18 Not all dioceses responded, and it has not proved possible to build up a complete picture, although it is clear from the information received that assistance from internal trusts and funds held by dioceses play a significant role in supporting clergy. Most of these payments appeared to be means-tested, and the amounts involved and the numbers of clergy receiving assistance varied widely from diocese to diocese. The figures we received are not complete, but suggest that around £250,000 was made available to about 1,200 clergy.

9.19 The role of clergy charities is also immensely significant, and several of the clergy charities also made valuable responses to the consultation document. On the basis of the responses received, approximately £4.5 million was distributed in 1999 to around 3,600 clergy.

9.20 The Group wishes to take this opportunity to pay tribute to work done by clergy charities, something for which the Church will always be grateful.

9.21 How best to assist clergy will always be a question for the individual charities to decide in accordance with their particular trust deeds. **The results of the Group's work suggest that particular areas where we recommend charities might wish to consider focusing their assistance are likely to be the following:**

  i) reconsidering their investment policies to make loans to clergy to enable them to make provision for retirement housing (see the last section of Chapter 8);

 ii) providing assistance for clergy with children, particularly with a non-earning spouse or no spouse;

iii) assistance with paying off higher education tuition fees and student loans.

chapter 10
affordability

the present situation

10.1 The present national stipend policy suggests stipend levels to dioceses, adjusted by regional cost-of-living factors, which allow dioceses to set their Basic Stipend within a small band of 1.5% below to 2.5% above their Regional Stipend Benchmark. It is a policy which, on the surface, keeps stipends across the country within close limits. Further details of the present system are given in Chapter 6.

10.2 By and large, the policy has been successful and it is apparent that most dioceses wish to hold to what is seen as a national stipend system.

10.3 The policy has, however, never met with total acceptance. For many years it was the Diocese of Rochester that paid higher stipends than those recommended by the CSA. More recently the Diocese of Guildford has paid stipends above these recommendations, while stipends in the Dioceses of London and Chichester have fallen significantly below their Regional Stipend Benchmarks.

10.4 The estimated stipends bill for the year 2001/02 was approximately £176.5 million (including employers' National Insurance but not pensions contributions). This was funded from the following sources:

Source	£ millions	
Church Commissioners	26.5	(15%)
Cathedrals	0.4	(0.2%)
Dioceses and parishes	133.8	(75.9%)
Parochial fees (Incumbents' fees)	14.3	(8.1%)
Other local income	1.4	(0.8%)
TOTAL	**176.5**	

the current financial state of the Church

10.5 The 1990s were a difficult time for the whole Church. The beginning of the decade saw the beginning of what was to be very substantial

reduction in the support made to dioceses by the Church
Commissioners for stipends and housing. The Commissioners, in
responding to requests within the Church, had taken on more
expenditure obligations than their investments could support in the
long term. In order to bring their expenditure down in line with their
income, they introduced a programme of reductions in stipends
support totalling £45 million p.a. over the period 1992 to 1997. This
was equivalent to a reduction of some £4,500 p.a. per minister.

10.6 The Lambeth Group was set up by the Archbishop of Canterbury to consider
the financial circumstances of the Church Commissioners. Its report,
issued in 1993, concluded that the Commissioners' assets were only
just sufficient to meet their pension liabilities with the consequence
that they could not continue to meet the full cost of clergy pensions
unless they stopped all other expenditure. This prompted the creation
of the new pension arrangements. The Commissioners would pay for all
pensions earned up to 1998 and a new scheme would fund the costs
of all pensions earned from 1998 onwards.

10.7 To help dioceses meet the cost of the pension scheme introduced in
1998, the Church Commissioners agreed to provide transitional
assistance to dioceses over the period 1998–2002 on a phased
basis. In 2000, this assistance amounted to £11.2 million. The net
amount of pension contributions payable by dioceses in 2000/01 was
approximately £20 million.

10.8 The recent actuarial review of the new clergy pension scheme, which
reported in April 2001, has suggested that the Church will need to
find an additional £12 million per annum to fund the current pensions
arrangements. The cost to the dioceses will be in the order of
£11 million for the pension costs of those clergy whose stipends
are paid by the dioceses. The period of traditional support by the
Commissioners has been extended to 2004 to help dioceses,
particularly the needier dioceses, to phase in this increase.

10.9 The most recent in-depth survey of the financial health of the Church
of England dates from October 2000. That report concluded that
dioceses had run in surplus between 1994 and 1997, but that overall
there was no surplus in 1998 and there was a deficit in 1999. It is
almost certain that during the earlier years dioceses retained a higher
number of posts than they were realistically going to fill, and that this
factor gave rise to the surpluses evident in the various financial reports.

10.10 The financial forecasts made by dioceses at the time gave cause for
concern. Thirty-six dioceses predicted annual deficits over the period
2001 to 2003 averaging between 2% and 10% per annum, whilst

only two predicted surpluses. The remaining ten forecasts were near to breakeven. The overall deficit was forecast at about £10 million p.a. Parishes recorded overall surpluses of £41 million in 1998 and £16 million in 1999.

10.11 In contrast, there has been a heartening increase in giving which rose during the period 1990–1999 from around £4 per person per week to nearly £7 per person per week. In real terms, taking inflation into account, this is an increase of 52%. Nevertheless, giving is still well below the General Synod's target of 5% of take-home pay.

10.12 In 2000 the new Gift Aid scheme was launched which should allow tax recovery on giving to be made more easily than under the previous scheme of covenanted giving. The Government announced in 2000 that the rate of VAT paid on repairs to listed buildings would be reduced from 17.5% to 5%. This should result in a saving to the Church of at least £10 million per annum. These changes will however take time to affect the overall pattern of the Church's finances.

10.13 In addition, the numbers of ordained stipendiary ministers in the Church of England has declined over recent years. Despite recent welcome increases in ordination candidates this trend will continue for the foreseeable future. As indicated in the supplementary report to *Managing Planning Growth* (CHP, 2001), stipendiary clergy numbers are projected to decline by 1% p.a. over the next decade, if the average number ordained to stipendiary ministry each year remains at 300. This will result in time in savings on the total stipend bill of approximately £17.5 million (excluding pension contributions).

10.14 It is clear that there are no great hidden reserves that could be unleashed to pay for substantial stipend increases and that any increases will have to be funded in the future, as in the past, by increased giving. What is affordable in any diocese will depend on the confidence in the ability of the parishes to engender further increased giving. In some dioceses this confidence will be greater than in others.

10.15 In their responses to the CSA consultation on the level of clergy stipends for 2002/03, 18 dioceses specifically mentioned affordability as a reason for not proposing higher stipends.

10.16 In response to the clergy survey, 3,530 clergy (56% of all respondents) replied that, in their opinion, their parishes could not afford a higher stipend than the present one.

10.17   The wealth of individual dioceses, both potential and real, varies considerably. The present situation in the Diocese of Guildford highlights the fact that what is considered affordable in one diocese is considered out of reach by the majority of other dioceses.

the Group's aspirations for change

10.18   **We recommend the following hierarchy of aspirations:**

i)   The first of these would be to bring the basic level of stipend for all assistant staff (including licensed lay workers) up to the National Minimum Stipend. The cost of doing this on the basis of 2001/02 figures would be just above £200,000.

ii)   The second aspiration would be to increase the National Stipend Benchmark from its current level of 1.05 of the National Minimum Stipend to 1.1 of the National Minimum Stipend. The cost of doing this on the basis of 2001/02 figures would be £5.0 million.

iii)   The third aspiration would be to pay all incumbents a stipend of £20,000, equivalent, with housing included, to approximately 80% of the starting-point salary of the primary school head teacher as described in Chapter 3. The total cost of doing this, starting from 2001/02 as a base, would be £28.5 million excluding pension contributions. (The additional cost after meeting aspirations (i) and (ii) would be £23.3 million.) Details of how all costings have been calculated are set out in **Appendix 7**.

iv)   The fourth aspiration would be the adoption of one of the stipends structures described in Chapter 5.

10.19   These additional costs have to be taken alongside the increase in pension contributions in order to gauge the affordability, diocese by diocese.

guaranteed annuities

10.20   Under the Endowments and Glebe Measure 1976, the Church Commissioners are statutorily bound to pay a 'Guaranteed Annuity' of £1,000.08 each year towards the stipend of the incumbent of a benefice. In making a response to the Group's Consultation Document, they asked for reactions to their proposal to abolish Guaranteed Annuities in line with their key strategic objective to increase the amount of money available for parish ministry in areas of need and opportunity. In 1978, when the Measure took effect,

Guaranteed Annuities accounted for 32% of the average incumbent's stipend. They now account for only 6%. They are made irrespective of needs or resources of the parish or the diocese concerned. They are cumbersome to administer and, if abolished, could release £5 million, which could be redirected to parishes where it was most needed. **Whilst recognizing that this issue remains under discussion between the Commissioners and the Archbishops' Council, the Group expressed the hope that legislation would be introduced to abolish Guaranteed Annuities but with the caveat that the money released should be used only to support stipends.**

conclusion

10.21 The base from which any stipend increase can be paid must be increased giving. Raising the money to increase the stipends of the clergy is not only a financial challenge to each diocese, but a spiritual one. If giving within the Church were at the recommended level of 5%, there would not be any need for the discussion on affordability.

10.22 As things stand at present, there will be many dioceses who, whilst sympathetic to the aim of improving clergy conditions, will find themselves unable to afford to lift stipends from their current levels without help from wealthier parts of the Church. This presents a challenge to the Church, as a national Church, to be far more willing than it has been to share the financial burden. The reality of our proposals is that their implementation may require further mutual support between dioceses. The principle of mutual support has been broadly welcomed, but there remain many difficulties between that broad agreement and its detailed acceptance and implementation.

appendix 1

consultation document and responses

consultation document

The Archbishops' Council has commissioned a major review of stipends paid to clergy and licensed lay workers. This is in response to concerns within the Church about whether stipends are adequate, and also about how stipends are to be funded, now that an increasing proportion of the stipends bill is being met from the current giving of lay people. The Group's terms of reference are set out on the last page. It is hoped that this document will be discussed widely throughout the Church by clergy, lay people, PCCs and other interested groups. The Group is also conducting a survey of all those people on the central payroll, held by the Church Commissioners, who are in receipt of stipends.

Note: Chaplains to prisons and the armed forces are paid salaries by the Home Office and the Ministry of Defence. Most full-time hospital chaplains and some university chaplains are paid by NHS Trusts and universities respectively. Their remuneration levels do not form part of this review.

comments are particularly invited on the following issues:

1. **the concept of the stipend**

2. **the level of the stipend**

3. **the use of differentials**

4. **the setting of stipends**

5. **other elements in the remuneration package**

6. **how any increases in stipends might be funded.**

the concept of the stipend

1. The majority of clergy and licensed lay workers receive stipends. The stipend has been variously described as '... not a reward but rather a means of releasing someone to give all of their time to the ministry ...' and 'an allowance or contribution designed to maintain a person who has chosen to follow a particular calling or vocation'. In 1943 the House of Bishops made the following statement about stipends:

   The stipends of the clergy have always, we imagine, been rightly regarded not as pay in the sense in which that word is understood in the world of industry today, not as a reward for services rendered, so that the more valuable the service in somebody's judgement or the more hours worked the more should be the pay, but rather as a maintenance allowance to enable the priest to live without undue financial worry, to do his work effectively in the sphere to which he is called and if married to maintain his wife and bring up his family in accordance with a standard which might be described as that neither of poverty nor riches.

2. This definition was framed at a time when all clergy were male, most clergy wives did not work outside the home and there were no clergy couples. A consultation on clergy conditions of service undertaken in 1994 indicated a large measure of support for the spirit of this definition, particularly as far as equal stipends for all incumbents are concerned. There is a debate in the Church about whether differentials should be paid to dignitaries. As recently as 1996 the General Synod voted against the abolition of such differentials. There is a view that they might be paid to other clergy as well.

the level of the stipend and how it is set

3. The stipends of parochial clergy and licensed lay workers are set by the dioceses, on the basis of recommendations from the Archbishops' Council in its role as Central Stipends Authority (CSA). Details of the CSA's recommendations for 2000/01 are shown at the end of this document. More details are contained in the CSA report for 1999, which is available on request from the Ministry Division (address below).

4. Recommendations by the CSA for increases in stipends are made after detailed consultation with dioceses. One aim of the CSA is to encourage the maintenance of a nationally coherent stipends

system. This reflects the self-understanding of the Church of England as being a national church. Broad conformity of stipends between dioceses is also seen as important in enabling clergy mobility throughout the country.

5. Each year the CSA recommends a National Stipend Benchmark for clergy of incumbent status. This is then adjusted to take account of regional variations in the cost of living using data from the Reward Group on comparative costs of a standard 'basket of goods' in nine different regions. The aim of such regional adjustment is to give clergy parity of purchasing power irrespective of their geographical location. Dioceses are encouraged to pay stipends not more than 2.5% above and not less than 1.5% below their Regional Stipend Benchmark. In all but a few dioceses, the greatest number of clergy of incumbent status in the diocese receive a stipend within this range.

6. The CSA also recommends a National Minimum Stipend for incumbents; no incumbent should be paid less than this for full-time ministry. This is increased each year by the same percentage as the National Stipend Benchmark and is used to calculate pension levels for clergy.

7. The CSA tracks the changes in clergy stipends against changes in the Retail Price Index and the Average Earnings Index. It also compares the purchasing power of clergy stipends with disposable incomes available to certain other professional groupings. This is done to provide a general indication of the adequacy of the stipend.

8. The CSA recommends a scale for assistant staff (including lay workers) with annual increases during the first four years of ministry, and additional payments for seniority or responsibility. Details are given at the end of the document.

9. The CSA also recommends to dioceses a stipend for archdeacons and makes recommendations to the Church Commissioners about the stipends paid to bishops, deans and provosts, and residentiary canons. Neither the stipends paid to dignitaries nor those paid to assistant staff nor pensions are adjusted regionally.

10. Dioceses employ a number of clergy in sector ministry posts such as directors of education or youth officers. They may be paid

either a salary or a stipend. Accommodation may be provided for them or they may receive a housing allowance.

other elements in the remuneration package

11. On retirement at or after the minimum normal pension age (65 for both women and men), clergy who have completed at least 37 years' pensionable service receive, in addition to their state pensions, a church pension of two-thirds of the previous year's National Minimum Stipend for incumbents plus a lump sum of three times the pension. The pension and lump sum for those with less than 37 years of qualifying service are proportionate.

12. The Church Commissioners are responsible for funding pensions arising from service before 1 January 1998. Under the new pension arrangements, the cost of pensions for service by parochial clergy after that date is funded by contributions from dioceses and parishes. Because of the link between the National Minimum Stipend and the pension (see paragraph 6) increases in the CSA's recommendations for stipends directly affect the cost of pensions for both past and future service.

13. Clergy make no direct contribution towards the cost of their pensions. If they were to make contributions, then stipends would need to rise to cover these payments and the National Insurance contributions which these increases would attract. The Church would also become liable for additional 'employer's contributions'.

14. Apart from the stipend and pension provision, the main element of the clergy remuneration package is the provision of housing (including the payment of Council tax, water charges, maintenance, external decorations and insurance). Although clergy do not have to pay these costs, it should be noted that clergy are generally required by virtue of their office to live in the accommodation provided for them, and thus have no choice about where they live. Clergy also have to provide accommodation for themselves and their families on retirement. The formula for calculating the pension and lump sum takes this into account and additional help with buying or renting retirement housing is available on a discretionary basis. Approximately one third of retired clergy make use of this. Clergy are also eligible for removal grants, subsidised motor and household contents

insurance in high-risk areas, and car loans at a concessionary rate of interest.

Please send your responses to the Clergy Stipends Review, Room 263, Ministry Division, Church House, Great Smith Street, London SW1P 3NZ by **30 September 2000**.

terms of reference

(i) To consider the concept and definition of the stipend;

(ii) to examine the content of the clergy remuneration package (including retirement provision) and its comparability with remuneration for other groups;

(iii) to ascertain, through a properly conducted large-scale survey of clergy and consultations with dioceses and charities, the financial circumstances of clergy;

(iv) to review the size of dignitaries' differentials;

(v) in conjunction with the Finance Committee, to evaluate the affordability and long-term financial sustainability of the present arrangements and any proposals for change;

(vi) to consider the implications of any proposals for:

clergy deployment and partnership between dioceses;

future numbers of stipendiary clergy and patterns of ministry;

(vii) to consider whether the present structure for setting stipends should be retained and outline possible alternative structures;

(viii) to consult with the Church Commissioners, the Pensions Board and dioceses;

(ix) to consult with other national church bodies through the Churches Main Committee and government agencies on matters of fiscal and taxation policy which affect stipends, in particular the treatment of benefits in kind;

(x) to determine options for wide debate within the Church.

the CSA's recommendations for 2000/2001

recommendations to dioceses for incumbents and clergy of incumbent status:

(i) A National Stipend Benchmark of £16,420

(ii) Regional Stipend Benchmarks for each diocese at a level between £15,750 and £16,810

(iii) A National Minimum Stipend for Incumbents of £15,570.

assistant staff and licensed lay workers: a stipend between £14,680 and £15,820 according to length of service, responsibility or personal circumstances.

archdeacons: a stipend of £24,630.

recommendations to the Church Commissioners

Residentiary Canons	£20,200
Deans and Provosts	£24,790
Suffragan Bishops	£24,790
Diocesan Bishops	£30,120
Bishop of London	£45,480
Archbishop of York	£48,770
Archbishop of Canterbury	£55,660

responses

The Group is grateful for the evidence received from the following individuals and groups:

bishops and retired bishops

The Rt Revd the Bishop of Blackburn*
The Rt Revd the Bishop of Chester*
The Rt Revd the Bishop of Peterborough*
The Rt Revd the Bishop of Ripon & Leeds*
The Rt Revd the Bishop of St Albans*
The Rt Revd the Bishop of Winchester*
The Rt Revd the Bishop of Repton
The Rt Revd the Bishop of Southampton
The Rt Revd the Bishop of Woolwich*
The Rt Revd Dr John Baker
The Rt Revd Dr Eric Kemp
The Rt Revd K. J. Woollcombe

deans and provosts

The Very Revd Dr John Arnold*
The Very Revd Nicholas Bury*
The Rt Revd Dr Rupert Hoare
The Very Revd Alec Knight
The Very Revd John Methuen
The Very Revd George Nairn-Briggs*
The Very Revd Michael Perham*
The Very Revd John Petty
The Very Revd Edward Shotter*

archdeacons

The Archdeacon of Aston
The Archdeacon of Basingstoke
The Archdeacon of Berkshire
The Archdeacon of Bradford
The Archdeacon of Bolton*
The Archdeacon of Cleveland
The Archdeacon of Colchester
The Archdeacon of East Riding
The Archdeacon of Halifax
The Archdeacon of Liverpool
The Archdeacon of Malmesbury*

The Archdeacon of Manchester
The Archdeacon of Middlesex*
The Archdeacon of Newark*
The Archdeacon of Northolt
The Archdeacon of Northumberland*
The Archdeacon of Sheffield
The Archdeacon of West Cumberland
The Archdeacon of Wiltshire
The Archdeacon of Winchester
The Archdeacon of York
The Ven. D. A. Rogers (retired)

other clergy

The Revd Derek Akker
The Revd H. O. Alby
The Revd Canon Ted Angus
The Revd Graeme Arthur
The Revd Canon Vincent Ashwin
The Revd Lionel Atherton
The Revd Ian Aveyard
The Revd Canon David Bailey*
The Revd David Barnes
The Revd James Barnett
The Revd Alan Bartlam
The Revd Alain Beardsmore
The Revd Canon Jeffrey Bell
The Revd Steven Betts*
The Revd Christopher Bindloss
The Revd David R. Bird*
The Revd Ian Black
The Revd Paul Boughton
The Revd Hugh Broad
The Revd Dr Neil Burgess
The Revd Dr Geoffrey Burn
The Revd Richard Burton
The Revd William Butt
The Revd Canon Douglas Caiger
The Revd Mark Cannon
The Revd Bruce Carlin
The Revd Canon Derek Carpenter
The Revd J. A. Cheeseman
The Revd Canon Peter Clark
The Revd Peter Clay
The Revd Paul Clemence
The Revd Jeremy Collingwood
The Revd M. Connell

The Revd Tim Cook
The Revd John Cooper
The Revd Michael Cooper
The Revd R. W. Cotton
The Revd Mike Cottrell
The Revd Andrew Couch
The Revd Derek E. Cowie
The Revd Paul Crabb
The Revd Canon Helen Cunliffe
The Revd Alyson Davie
The Revd Kevin Davies
The Revd Tim Daykin
The Revd Eric Delve
The Revd Anne Donaldson
The Revd Dr Edgar Dowse
The Revd D. J. Duncanson
The Revd Michael Dykes
The Revd Stephen Earl
The Revd Andrew Edwards
The Revd Robert Ellis*
The Revd Stuart A. Evason
The Revd J. M. S. Falkner
The Revd Canon Pamela Fawcett
The Revd Paul Fiske
The Revd Stephen Fletcher
The Revd Dr David B. Foss
The Revd Simon Foulkes
The Revd Canon David Fowler
The Revd James J. Gill
The Revd Ian E. Gooding
The Revd Matthew Grayshon
The Revd Peter Guinness
The Revd William Halling

other clergy contd

The Revd C. D. Harrison
The Revd R. Hart
The Revd Roger J. Hoare
The Revd Canon Michael Hodge
The Revd Timothy Horsington
The Revd Paul Hunt
The Revd Gary Ingram
The Revd L. S. Ireland
The Revd Canon David Ison
The Revd Canon Ian Jagger
The Revd Mark Johnson
The Revd Canon P. F. Johnson
The Revd Vic Johnson
The Revd Nick Jones
The Revd Peter Kelly
The Revd Malcolm King
The Revd Paul Knight
The Revd William Lamb
The Revd M. R. Land
The Revd Michael Lewis
The Revd Chris Lilley*
The Revd Philip Littlewood
The Revd Bruce Lyons
The Revd Canon Donald Macdonald
The Revd Donald MacGregor
The Revd David Macha
The Revd Christopher Malkinson
The Revd Canon Hugh Marshall
The Revd Rupert Martin
The Revd David Mayhew
The Revd John Mills and Mrs S. Mills
The Revd David Monteith
The Revd Raymond Morris
The Revd Stephen Mourant
Father David Mumford
The Revd Tim Newcombe*
The Revd Canon James Newcome*
The Revd C. Norman
The Revd Canon Gordon Oliver*
The Revd Robert Orchin
The Revd David Ottley
The Revd Canon Stephen Palmer
The Revd Canon Trevor Page
The Revd Canon Dr Trevor Park
The Revd Canon Marlene Parsons

The Revd Michael and Mrs Nia Pearson
The Revd Canon Dr Martyn Percy
The Revd John Pilkington
The Revd Robert J. Pimm
The Revd James Pitkin
The Revd Francis Pole
The Revd John Porter
The Revd Canon Keith Punshon
The Revd Nicholas Ralph
The Revd Peter Rapsey
The Revd M. D. Ratcliffe
The Revd Edward Rennard
The Revd E. M. Rew
The Revd Charles Richardson
The Revd Canon Jim Richardson
The Revd David Robbins
The Revd Frank Robinson
The Revd Dr Judith Rose
The Revd John Routh
The Revd John Russell
The Revd David Ryan
The Revd Peter Sainsbury
The Revd E. Sewell
The Revd Mike Sheffield
The Revd Geoffrey Shilvock
The Revd G. D. Simmons
The Revd John Smart
The Revd C. F. Smith
The Revd David S. M. Smith
The Revd D. Stevenson
The Revd Canon Charles Stewart
The Revd David and Mrs Pauline
  Stocker
The Revd Michael Storey
The Revd Nigel Strafford
The Revd Trevor Stubbs
The Revd Geoffrey H. Suart
The Revd Peter Swales
The Revd J. Brian Swallow
The Revd Graham Sykes
The Revd Alan Taylor
The Revd Jeremy Tear
The Revd Canon Nicholas
  Thistlethwaite
The Revd Andrew M. Thomson

other clergy contd

The Revd David R. Tilley
The Revd Nick Todd
The Revd Roger Trumper
The Revd Andrew Wadsworth
The Revd Peter Wadsworth
The Revd Robert B. Watson
The Revd Michael Webb*
The Revd Canon Jim Wellington*
The Revd Philip Welsh
The Revd Philip West
The Revd Martin Weymont

The Revd R. N. Whittingham
The Revd Canon G. T. Willett
The Revd Canon David Williams
The Revd D. Williams
The Revd Dr John Williams
The Revd J. N. O. Williams
The Revd David Wilmot
The Revd Frances Wookey
The Revd John Wright
The Revd Frank Wright
The Revd Paul Yiend

lay people

Mr T. R. Adams
Odette Amor
Mrs G. Ashworth
Mr Michael Ayles
Mrs Jessie Axtell
Ms Sallie Bassham*
Mr John K. Bellamy
Mr R. W. Berrill
Dr D. R. Blackmore
Mr Andrew Britton
Dr John W. Bull*
Mrs Elaine Bullock
Mrs Annie Clacey
Mr Robin Clough
Mr John Cooper
Mr Paul Cooper
Judy Ekins
Mr H. G. Ellison
Mr Ian Fawkner
Mr Jonathan Goll
Mr J. C. Hayes
Mr T. A. Harris
Mr A. J. Hutchinson
Mr S. L. Josephs
Mr David Kemp
Mr Edward Kidd
The Rt Hon. Lord Kingsdown KG
Mr Clifford and Mrs Eileen Lake
Mr Ben Laite

Mrs Elizabeth Lloyd
Mrs Sally Lowe
Mr Philip Mallet
Mr A. Mayer
Mrs E. Meredith
Mr R. A. Miller
Michael Oakley
Mrs E. B. Painter
Mr John Ramuz
Mrs Janet Reynolds
Mr K. Robinson
Mr Lyndon Sheppard
Mr M. D. Smith
Mrs J. Spinks
Mr Geoffrey Streets
Mr W. H. Taylor*
Jill Thake
Mr Peter Thornton
John Tillotson
Mr Ralph Tuck
Mr L. Twining
Hilary Unsworth
Mrs P. M. Wadge
Mr Peter Wedderburn-Ogilvy
Ms Leonie Wheeler
Mrs Shirley-Ann Williams*
Mrs Janet Woodger
Mr Charles Wylie

*denotes membership of General Synod from November 2000.

theological colleges and courses

St John's College Nottingham
The Principal, Southern Theological and Educational Training Scheme

The Principal, Westcott House
The Principal, St Stephens House

corporate responses

Archbishop's Council, Diocese of Canterbury
Bishops and Archdeacons of the Diocese of London
Bishop of Birmingham's Council
Bishop's Council, Diocese of Bath and Wells
Bishop's Council, Diocese of Ely
Bishops Waltham Deanery Synod
Broken Rites
Chapter, Bisley Deanery, Gloucestershire
Chapter, Campden Deanery, Warwickshire
Chapter, Frome Deanery Synod
Chapter, Hawkesbury Deanery Synod, Thornbury
Chapter, Newcastle Central Deanery
Church Commissioners
Congregation of St George's Church, Kendal
Deanery Synod, Chorley
Diocesan Board of Finance, Chichester
Diocesan Board of Finance Durham
Diocesan Board of Finance, Liverpool
Diocesan Board of Finance, Portsmouth
Diocesan Board of Finance, Southwell
Diocesan Board of Finance, Worcester
English Clergy Association
Executive Committee, Diocesan Board of Finance, Diocese of Norwich
Finance and Central Services Committee, Diocesan Board of Finance, Diocese of Chester
Friends of the Clergy Corporation
Lincoln Diocesan Stipends and Conditions of Service Committee

MSF
PCC, All Saints' Church, Bubwith and Aughton, North Yorkshire
PCC, All Saints Pavement with St Crux and St Michael Spurriergate, York
PCC, Chapel of Ease, St Alban-the-Martyn, Upper Ventnor
PCC, Froxfield with Privett, Portsmouth
PCC, Holy Trinity, Ventnor
PCC, Marden
PCC, St Andrew's Church Swanwick
PCC, St Gregory's Church, Cropton, Pickering
PCC, St Helen's Church, Skipwith, Yorkshire
PCC, St James The Apostle, Selby
PCC, St John the Evangelist, Old Trafford
PCC, St John the Evangelist Church, Yeadon
PCC, St Luke's Church, Maidstone, Kent
PCC, St Martin Norris Bank, Stockport
PCC, St Mary and All Saints, Boxley
PCC, St Mary's Church, Brighstone and Mottistone with Brook
PCC, St Mary and All Saints, Chesterfield
PCC, St Mary's Parish Church, Moston
PCC, St Mary's Church, Portchester
PCC, St Mary's Parish Church, Thirsk, North Yorkshire
PCC, St Matthew, Blackmoor and Whitehill
PCC, St Nicholas Church, Hull
PCC, St Peter's Elmton, St Mary Magdalene Creswell

corporate responses contd

PCC, St Peter's Church, Norton,
North Yorkshire

PCC, St Peter's Church, Redcar

PCC, St Werburgh's Parish Church,
Chorlton-cum-Hardy

The lay members of the PCC
of the parish of Holy Trinity,
Ventnor

Representatives of the Diocese of
Peterborough

Retired Clergy Association

St Alphege Church, District Church
Council, Sea Salter

St Mary's District Church Council

Staff Committee, Leicester Diocesan
Board of Finance

Standing Committee, House of
Clergy, Diocese of Carlisle

The Management Sub-Committee
and Diocesan Board of Finance,
Sheffield

The Sub-Committee of the District
Church Council of Whitstable

appendix 2

responses from charitable organizations and dioceses

responses from charitable organizations

Responses were received from the following charitable organizations in response to a request for information regarding the funds distributed to clergy in 1999.

The Church of England Clergy Stipend Trust

City Parochial Foundation

Corporation of the Sons of the Clergy

The English Clergy Association

Frances Ashton's Charity

The Friends of the Clergy Corporation

Hospital of God at Gretham

Lord Crewe's Charity

Pyncombe Charity

The Queen Victoria Clergy Fund

Royal St Ann's Society

Smith's Charity

Society for the Relief of Poor Clergymen

Tranquillity House

responses from dioceses

Responses were received from the following dioceses/bishops in response to a request for information regarding payments made to clergy within the diocese in 1999.

Bath & Wells

Birmingham

Blackburn

Bradford

Canterbury

Carlisle

Chester

Gloucester

Guildford

Leicester

Lincoln

Liverpool

Manchester

Manchester

Newcastle

Norwich

Oxford

Portsmouth

Ripon & Leeds

St Albans

St Edmundsbury & Ipswich

Salisbury

Sheffield

Southwell

Truro

Wakefield

Winchester

York

appendix 3

the Tearfund system of remuneration

This appendix describes a salary-based approach which is not untypical of a number of similar models used by 'caring' based charities, e.g. Oxfam, Save The Children Fund, Tearfund, World Vision, Christian Aid, etc. Their reward systems reflect the values both of the organization and those working for them. By way of an example, and with its agreement, the following sets out how Tearfund, a Christian international relief and development organization, operates its remuneration policy.

Tearfund's philosophy on pay

- *Committed to Christ*
  - acknowledging Christ as Lord and being obedient to his will
  - following his example of sacrificial love and service
  - acknowledging their dependence upon Christ's grace and power

- *Committed to accountability*
  - for use of time and resources
  - to partners and supporters by being honest, trustworthy and transparent
  - to make actions consistent with what they say

- *Committed to excellence*
  - quality of service in a professional way to partners, supporters and colleagues

main objectives of Tearfund's remuneration policy

- remuneration to reflect mission, values and strategy;
- internally equitable and consistent with relative salaries by being logically based on rational decisions;
- simple to understand, explain, administer and manage;
- open, owned and felt fair by staff;
- cost-effective, providing quality/value for money – within budget;
- to reflect the content and responsibility of individual roles;
- to attract and retain staff with the 'right' skills;
- to balance the ethical issue of serving the poor with the need to reward staff fairly;
- to encourage flexibility in roles and team working.

remuneration policy

In developing its policy three years ago, Tearfund considered various options. It adopted a broad banding approach which optimizes flexibility within wide but clearly defined salary ranges. Certain criteria are applied to give guidance within the salary ranges or broad bands.

Tearfund compared its salaries with three market groups, i.e. international aid agencies, missionary organizations and the local market (local business and employers). As a result it aims to set salaries between the middle and lower range of international aid agencies, and the higher end of missionary organizations, and for lower paid jobs the local market rate (in and around its Teddington HQ).

Five 'market related' broad salary ranges cover most of the jobs:

> Group leader
> Team leader
> Team member 1
> Team member 2
> Team member 3.

remuneration process

Step 1 – Decision on the band a job is to be placed in is made by the line manager and personnel unit, based on the definitions set out for the grade

Step 2 – Decision on salary is based on the skills and experience the job holder brings to the post, looked at in the light of other posts

Decision on salaries within the range are based on:

Market match comparison
Experience/expertise.

There are set amounts allowed for differentials to reflect levels of experience/expertise according to salary band:

Band A – £300
Band B – £750
Band C – £1000
Band D – over £1000 p.a.

The following is a worked example:

If a post within Band B Team member (2) had a match in the local market of around £13,000 p.a. then the Group Leader/Team Leader in conjunction with personnel would have the discretion to place the salary at £375 p.a. above or below this level, i.e. £12,625 to £13,375 p.a.

annual increases in salary

A percentage 'across-the-board' increase is agreed for all staff each year. Progression through a salary band would come through job change or promotion and would not be related directly to individual level of performance.

appendix 4

Central Stipends Authority recommendations for 2001/02

recommendations to dioceses

incumbents and clergy of incumbent status

(a) A National Stipend Benchmark of £16,910

(b) Regional Stipend Benchmarks for each diocese at a level between £16,610 and £17,330

(c) A National Minimum stipend of £16,040.

assistant staff

Assistant curates, deacons, deaconesses and licensed lay workers (including Church Army evangelists engaged in the parochial ministry) are all regarded as assistant staff for the purposes of stipends.

Year 1	£15,120
Year 2	£15,370
Year 3	£15,590
Year 4	£15,810
Additional points + Point A	
for seniority or	£16,050
Responsibility + Point B	£16,290

The additional points in the scale above should be used with flexibility in those cases where the varying needs and circumstances of individual clergy are not met by the annual incremental part of the scale, e.g. the older minister, recently ordained, with family commitments, those with greater seniority or perhaps exceptional experience or responsibility. Dioceses will, as now, be free to pay more where individual or local circumstances justify it.
archdeacons

A stipend of £25,370.

related conditions

1. **Definition of Income**: stipends are to be calculated in accordance with the method of computing income for augmentation purposes approved by the General Synod at its February Group of Sessions 1975 (see **Appendix 6**).

2. **Accommodation**: this should be provided free of rent, water charges, repairs and insurance and the Council tax; or an adequate allowance should be paid instead.

3. **Approved parochial expenses**: these should be fully reimbursed.

minimum resettlement (and removal) grants

These are recommended minimum grants, and are payable in addition to the cost of removal ('the van').

	Resettlement i.e. moving in	First Appointment Grant (payable in addition to resettlement grants)
Group A (Archdeacons and ministers of incumbent status)	At least £1,600	At least £1,600
Group B (Assistant curates, deacons,deaconesses and licensed lay workers)	At least £1,510	At least £1,360

The grants for Group A represent 10% of the National Minimum Stipend. The grants for Group B represent 10% and 9% respectively of year 1 of the National Scale for assistant staff.

recommendations to the Church Commissioners

Archbishop of Canterbury	£57,320
Archbishop of York	£50,220
Bishop of London	£46,840
Diocesan Bishops	£31,110
Suffragan Bishops	£25,530
Assistant Bishops (full-time)	£24,520
Deans and Provosts	£25,530
Residentiary Canons	£20,800

appendix 5 the remuneration of clergy in other churches

	The Methodist Church	The United Reformed Church	The Baptist Church
Stipend	Basic stipend – 2001/02 £14,940	Basic Stipend – 2001 £16,944 Children's allowances of £800 p.a. for first child, £400 p.a. paid for additional dependent children up to 24 years old, some restrictions apply	Each local church is responsible for employing its own minister locally and for paying the stipend agreed between minister and church. Churches that are not able to pay are assisted with grants to bring stipends up to Home Mission Standard Stipend of £14,600 in 2001. Many non-aided churches pay above the Home Mission Standard Stipend
Pensions	Ministers contribute 6% of stipend	Ministers under 55 may join the URC Ministers Pension Fund. Ministers over 55 have contributions paid to a fund of their choice Retirement age 65	Ministers can join the Baptist Ministers Pension Scheme and contribute 5% of stipend. The Church contributes 10% of stipend
Housing	Provided or housing allowance paid	Provided or housing allowance paid	Provided by local church or housing allowance paid to minister living in own house
Differentials	Between 5% and 25% of basic stipend for certain posts	None	No structured differentials
Other elements in remuneration package	Fees retained by ministers Removal expenses paid by local church or circuit One-off loan of £5,000 for car or office equipment or furniture and furnishings Initial grant of £1,850 maximum (if assets below £6,000) Sabbatical fund of £55 per minister per annum People may use up to £600 for a sabbatical Entitlement after 10 years then every 7 years. All essential expenditure met	Car provided by church where regular use considered necessary by church council Resettlement grant of £2,450 for initial post and subsequent moves Ordination loan of £2,450 Retirement removal grant of £1,225	Standard reimbursement of car mileage rates based on Inland Revenue Fixed Profit Car Scheme plus expenses of office Church normally pays for minister to attend the annual Assembly. Removal expenses normally met by church, with a contribution from the centre when a minister retires. Church normally pays manse telephone with private calls reimbursed
Holiday entitlement	35 days plus statutory public holidays	5 weeks in each calendar year and one additional Sunday. (More are allowed if the minister pays for pulpit supply.)	
Health care schemes			
Sick leave	Full stipend throughout any period of sickness		

	Roman Catholic Church	New Frontiers International
Stipend	Determined within each diocese and intended to cover personal expenditure. Priests not working in parish ministry usually receive a higher stipend than those in parishes.	Some churches use the Teachers and National Joint Council pay scales. Ministers set at Head of Year. Or The trustees select six or so typical church members and use the average of their incomes as the minister's salary.
Offerings	Priests also keep stole fees (offerings on the occasions of marriages, baptisms, weddings and funerals). Christmas and Easter offerings are traditionally for the priests of a parish. Priests also receive Mass stipends. (A priest may also accept an offering when he celebrates Mass.) Although a priest may celebrate Mass more than once a day, he may accept only one offering each day.	
Pensions	Priests usually retire at 75. Arrangements vary between dioceses on pensions. Most dioceses provide accommodation for a retired priest up to a determined sum or meet costs if he chooses to live in a presbytery. A retired priest receives a retirement allowance as well as allowances from clergy mutual funds.	A matter for local trustees
Housing	Priests are accommodated in parish houses. The houses are maintained from parish funds and sustenance provided. The personal aspects of this arrangement are a taxable liability for the individual priest.	Ministers provide their own housing
Differentials	There are no formal differentials, although income will depend on the nature of a priest's appointment at any given time. Some dioceses seek to minimize differentials by guaranteeing a minimum income to each priest.	
Other elements in the remuneration package	Travel expenses are met and the use by the priest of his own car at Inland Revenue non-liability rates. Relevant National Insurance contributions can be reclaimed from the diocese or parish.	In addition to usual expenses, some churches give book allowances and/or pay for attendance at conferences. Ministers are offered courses to prepare for retirement.
Holiday entitlement	One day per week off and an annual holiday entitlement of 30 days (usually regulated by the number of Sundays a priest is absent from his parish).	
Health care schemes	Most dioceses operate a health care scheme which is also a taxable benefit.	
Sick leave	Cover is provided by other priests when a colleague is on sick leave.	

	The Church in Wales	The Church in Ireland	The Scottish Episcopal Church
Stipend	Minimum Stipends (2001) Assistant Curate £13,523 Incumbent, Vicar in Rectorial Benefice or Cleric in Charge £15,909 Incumbent of Rectorial Benefice £16,705	National Minimum Approved Stipend (MAS) of £19,086 in 2001 Dioceses are asked not to exceed 110% MAS Curates are paid at 75% of MAS in year 1 rising to 85% after 5 years	A recent stipends review advocated that the standard stipend should be the same as the Church of England's NSB
Pensions	A full service pension of 60% of the highest pensionable office held in five years preceding retirement after 40 years. Non-contributory scheme	Full service pension of 40/60ths of MAS. Clergy may retire at 65 and must retire by 75	Non-contributory full-service pension of 40/80ths of standard stipend. Contracted in to SERPS
Housing	Value for 'free' accommodation agreed with Inland Revenue at £7000	Clergy are required to live within the parish in a provided house	Provided housing
Differentials	Related to incumbent's stipend as follows: Residentiary Canon 115% Archdeacon 153% Dean 155% Diocesan Bishop 185% Archbishop 200%	No statutory provision for Canons, Archdeacons or Deans but they may receive up to £2,500 above MAS Bishops receive 175% of MAS The Diocesan Bishops receive 225% of MAS, Archbishops 245%	Bishops receive 150% of standard stipend
Other Elements in the Remuneration Package	Car loan scheme Retirement Housing Loan Scheme: £15,000 loan at 6% to £30,000 equity loan at 0%	Car mileage reimbursed on public sector rate 'Expenses of office' allowance, e.g. telephone, etc. Determined by the Diocesan Council and set between £600–1,000.	Some dioceses operate car loan schemes. Car expenses reimbursed according to the Fixed Profits Car Scheme Child allowances for households with less than £20,000 income for children up to 18. £160 per child in 1999, to be index-linked in future.
Holiday entitlement			Four weeks basic holiday (including five Sundays) Six days following Christmas or Easter (flexible in consultation with the vestry)
Health care schemes			
Sick Leave			Any statutory sick pay received by clergy is to be deducted from stipend.

	The Church of Scotland	The Church of Sweden	The Anglican Church in New Zealand
Stipend	Minimum stipend for 2001 is £18,016 A service supplement is payable as follows: 5 years – £833 6 years – £1,666 7 years – £2,499 8 years – £3,333 9 years – £4,166	Negotiated between the regional branch of the trade union to which the minister belongs, taking into consideration the views of the head of the church board and the vicar.	Stipend is set at the average expenditure of a couple over 45 years old (as assessed by Statistics NZ)
Pensions	Ministers inducted since 1990 contribute 2% of stipend towards a money purchase scheme. Ministers inducted before 1990 pay less. Congregations pay 20% of stipend + 20% service supplement	3.5% of stipend set aside in a fund from age 28. Will yield 10% stipend in addition to state pension, equivalent to 55% of stipend	Ministers pay 6% of stipend
Housing	Housing is provided There is no alternative	Some parishes require their clergy to live in the parsonage house. Clergy pay rent which they would pay for an apartment of 100 square metres. Bishops have free housing	Ministers have housing provided but they pay tax on the 'value' of the vicarage, this being assessed as one-twelfth of their stipend. Some dioceses may pay a housing allowance if the minister wishes to live in his or her own home
Differentials			
Other elements in the Remuneration Package	In addition to car expenses (40p/mile less than 4000 miles, 22.5p/mile afterwards) plus £80 per month capital allowance		Expenses include travel and hospitality, books and periodicals, course fees, supervision and spiritual direction. Computer software may be included in this
Holiday entitlement			
Health care schemes			Most dioceses are in a scheme which offers a group subsidy of 20%
Sick Leave			There is a national Salary Continuance Scheme in place which provides 50% of stipend, tax free, for full disability, after a 3 month period of sick-leave. Clergy make a small contribution to premiums

	The Anglican Church in Australia	Ichthus Christian Fellowship	Army Chaplains
Stipend	Each diocese sets its own stipend. Commonly set at 70–75% average weekly earnings	In the range of £13,000 – £16,000 according to seniority and experience. Some leaders choose not to receive a salary	Paid according to rank and length of service From £27,783 on appointment to £53,983 after 26 years service (Classes 2, 3, 4)
Pensions	Clergy contribute through a variety of diocesan, parish or personal contributions to super-annuation funds	All are entitled to join pension scheme. Ichthus will match the employee's contribution up to 5% of their salary	Army chaplains may join the Armed Forces Pension Scheme
Housing	Housing is provided	Church workers responsible for their own housing	Housing provided at a subsidized rate for which chaplains pay rent
Differentials	Parishes allowed to pay above minimum rates as circumstances allow.	Senior leaders receive £16,000 and congregation leaders receive £15,000	Class 1 Rank (Colonel) – £53,983 Principal Chaplain – £57,169 Deputy Chaplain General (Brigadier) – £60,177 Chaplain General – £69,828
Other elements in the Remuneration Package		Mileage and telephone expenses paid up to a maximum of £150 per month and at a mileage rate of 28p per mile	Ministry of Defence funded car is provided
Holiday entitlement			
Health care schemes			
Sick Leave			

appendix 6

the method of computing income for augmentation purposes approved by the General Synod at its February Group of Sessions 1975

Income for this purpose will include:

Guaranteed Annuities and Personal Grants.[1]

Parochial giving direct for stipend (including contributions towards the cost of heating, lighting and cleaning the parsonage house).

Easter Offering.[2]

Fees (both parochial and non-parochial).

Net income from chaplaincies.[3]

Net income from public and education appointments.[3]

Income from local trusts.

The computation of income for augmentation purposes will not include:

Spare-time earnings.

Spouse's earnings.

Private income.

Income from the informal letting of parsonage house rooms. It will, however, be open to dioceses to make arrangements as regards the commercial letting of rooms on a significant scale (e.g. in holiday areas).

Nor will computation of income for augmentation purposes take account of payments for, or made in reimbursement of, approved working expenses.

appendix 7

costings of the proposals in the report

The stipends bill for the year 2001/02 is forecast to be approximately as follows:

Clergy	Estimated Number of clergy	Estimated Total stipend paid (£)
Assistant curates	1,700	27,081,000
Clergy on the diocesan basic stipend – the stipend paid to the greatest number of clergy of incumbent status in a diocese	6,444	109,422,855
Clergy of incumbent status receiving more than the diocesan basic stipend	1,007	17,763,626
Archdeacons	107	2,714,590
Clergy whose stipends are paid by the Church Commissioners	237	5,963,580
Others	34	577,320
TOTAL	9,529	163,522,972
Employer's National Insurance Contributions (Estimate based on actual amounts paid)		8,950,000
TOTAL	9,529	172,452,972

NB: these figures exclude part-time clergy and part-time lay workers, of whom there are approximately 400. The total stipend paid to them is around £3m p.a.

They also exclude approximately 130 full-time lay workers, who generally receive a higher stipend than the National Minimum Stipend for incumbents. The total stipend paid to them is around £2m p.a.

the Group's 'hierarchy of aspirations'

The following provisional costings are provided:

(i) cost of bringing assistant staff up to the 2001/02 National Minimum Stipend of £16,040;

(ii) cost of (a) increasing 2001 National Stipend Benchmark from current level of 1.05 of NMS (£16,910) to 1.1 of NMS (£17,640) and (b) applying this 4.3% increase to clergy currently above diocesan basic stipends;

(iii) cost of (a) increasing NSB to £20,000, (b) applying a 17.4% increase to clergy currently above diocesan basics, (c) bringing all assistant staff to the NMS of £18,200 and (d) assessing impact on pensions in following year;

(iv) cost of increasing dignitaries' stipends as suggested in chapter 4 to (a) dioceses and (b) the Church Commissioners.

It should be noted that the figures have been calculated only on a global basis and the impact of these proposals will vary from diocese to diocese.

(i) cost of bringing assistant staff up to the 2001/02 NMS of £16,040

Current figures suggest that the average stipend for assistant curates is between point 4 (£15,810) and additional point A (£16,050) of the 2001/02 scale for assistant staff, i.e. £15,930

2001 National Minimum Stipend for incumbents	£16,040
Estimated average for assistant curates	(£15,930)
Additional stipend required	£110

Cost of bringing up 1700 assistant curates to current NMS
£110 x 1700 = £187,000
Additional National Insurance Contributions at 8.2% of additional stipend £15,334

total additional cost of bringing all curates up to the NMS
£202,334

NB: the estimated average stipend for lay workers is already above the NMS.

(ii) cost of increasing the National Stipend Benchmark from 1.05 to 1.1 of current NMS at 2001/02 levels

(a) cost of increasing NSB from £16,910 (1.05 of NMS) to £17,640 (1.1 of NMS)

Proposed New NSB at 1.1 instead of 1.05 of NMS	£17,640
Projected national average stipend for 2001	(£17,030)
Required increase in NSB	£610

Note: the national average stipend has been used, as it is already £120 higher than the current NSB.

Number of Clergy on the Diocesan Basic Stipend 6,444

Cost of increasing NSB to 1.1 of NMS   £610 x 6,444 = £3,930,840

Additional National Insurance costs	£322,329
Additional costs	£4,253,169

(b) cost of applying an equivalent increase to clergy receiving more than the diocesan basic stipend

On the basis of previous trends, we have made an assumption that clergy receiving more than the diocesan basic stipend are already receiving on average 1.1 of NMS, i.e. £17,640.

Percentage increase in NSB if it is raised from £16,910 (1.05 of NMS) to £17,640 (1.1 of NMS) = 4.3%

Additional stipend for clergy above diocesan basic   4.3% x £17,640 = £758

Estimated number of clergy of incumbent status receiving more than diocesan basic stipend = 1,007

Cost of applying equivalent increase   £758 x 1,007 = £763,306

Additional National Insurance costs	£62,591
Additional costs	£825,897

total additional cost of increasing NSB from 1.05 to 1.1 of current NMS at 2001/02 levels £5,079,066

NB Aspirations (i) and (ii) do not result in any increase in the level of pension contributions.

(iii) cost of implementing Incumbent's Stipend Guideline of £20,000 and consequential increases

(a) cost of New Incumbent's Stipend Guideline

New Incumbent's Stipend Guideline	£20,000
Projected National Average Stipend	(£17,030)
Additional stipend required	£2,970
Estimated number of clergy on diocesan basic stipend	6,444

Cost of increasing NSB to £20,000 = £2,970 x 6,444 = £19,138,660

Additional National Insurance costs	£1,569,371
Additional costs	£20,708,031

(b) cost of applying an equivalent increase to clergy receiving more than the diocesan basic stipend

On the basis of previous trends, we have made an assumption that clergy receiving more than the diocesan basic stipend are already receiving on average 1.1 of NMS, i.e. £17,640.

Percentage increase if national average stipend (£17,030) increases to Incumbent's Stipend Guideline (£20,000) is 17.4%.

Additional stipend for clergy above diocesan basic
17.4% x £17,640 = £3,069
Estimated number of clergy of incumbent status receiving more than diocesan basic stipend 1,007

Cost of applying equivalent increase £3,069 x 1,007 =	£3,090,846
Additional National Insurance costs	£253,449
Additional costs	£3,344,295

(c) cost of the consequential increase in the NMS

If the new Incumbent's Stipend Guideline is at £20,000 and is 1.1 of NMS, the new NMS will be £18,180, say £18,200. This would be applied to assistant clergy.

New NMS	£18,200
2001/02 NMS	(£16,040)
Additional Stipend	£2,160

Estimated number of assistant curates 1,700

Cost of increasing NMS to £18,200   1,700 x 2160 = £3,672,000

Additional National Insurance costs   £301,104

Additional costs   £3,973,104

Total (parts a + b + c + cost of bringing archdeacons to new NMS and new differential – see note at (iv(a(ii))) below): £28,459,602

(d) additional amount of pension contributions paid by <u>dioceses</u> in the following year (2002/03)

	incumbents & assistants	archdeacons
29.1% of new NMS (£18,200)	£5,296	£6,220
29.1% of 2001/02 NMS (£16,040)	(£4,668)	(£5,835)
Additional pensions contributions per cleric	£628	£785
Total number of parochial diocesan clergy	9,151	107
Additional pension costs	£5,746,828	£83,995

Total (incumbents, assistants and archdeacons) – £5,830,823

The impact of these increases on the Church Commissioners and other bodies responsible for paying pension contributions has not been shown.

(iv) costs of increasing dignitaries' stipends using the new structure for differentials recommended in Chapter 4

(a) Archdeacons' stipends paid by dioceses

(i) cost of changing differential from 1.58 of current NMS to 1.6 of current NMS of £16,040

Proposed archdeacon's stipend of 1.6 of NMS	£25,670
Archdeacon's stipend in 2001/02 at 1.58 of NMS	(£25,370)
Additional stipend	£300
Number of archdeacons	107
Additional cost 107 x £300	£32,100
National Insurance costs	£2,632
Additional costs	£34,732

(ii) cost of changing differential from 1.58 of current NMS to 1.6 of new NMS on new NMS of £18,200

Proposed archdeacon's stipend of 1.6 of proposed NMS	£29,120
Current archdeacon's stipend 1.58 of current NMS	(£25,370)
Additional Stipend	£3,750
Number of archdeacons	107
Additional cost 107 x £3,750	£401,250
Additional National Insurance costs	£32,902
Additional costs	£434,152

(b) cost of dignitaries paid by Church Commissioners

NB: these figures assume no vacancies

Current Costs*

	number of clergy	current multiple of NMS	current cost with NMS @ £16,040
Assistant Bishops	1	1.52	24,520
Deans	41	1.59	1,046,730
Suffragan Bishops	68	1.59	1,736,040
Diocesan Bishops	41	1.94	1,275,510
Bishop of London	1	2.92	46,840
Archbishop of York	1	3.13	50,220
Archbishop of Canterbury	1	3.57	57,320
Total	–	–	4,212,660

*83 Residentiary Canons have been excluded from these calculations.

Cost of new differentials if NMS stays at current level of £16,040

	no.	new multiple of NMS	cost if NMS stays @ £16,040	increase on current costs
Deans	41	1.7	1,117,988	71,258
Suffragan Bishops	68	1.7	1,854,224	93,664
Diocesan Bishops	41	2.0	1,315,280	39,770
Bishop of London	1	3.0	48,120	1,280
Archbishop of York	1	3.25	52,130	1,910
Archbishop of Canterbury	1	3.75	60,150	2,830
Stipend Bill	–	–	**£4,447,892**	**£210,712**
Additional National Insurance costs	–	–		£17,278
Additional costs	–	–		**£227,990**

Cost of new differentials if NMS is increased to £18,200

	no.	new multiple of NMS	cost if NMS is increased to £18,200	increase on costs if NMS had remained at levels above
Deans	41	1.7	1,268,540	150,552
Suffragan Bishops	68	1.7	2,103,920	249,696
Diocesan Bishops	41	2.0	1,492,400	177,120
Bishop of London	1	3.0	54,600	6,480
Archbishop of York	1	3.25	59,150	7,020
Archbishop of Canterbury	1	3.75	68,250	8,100
Stipend Bill	–	–	**£5,046,860**	**£598,968**
Additional National Insurance costs	–	–		£49,115
Additional costs	–	–		**£648,083**

notes

chapter 2

1. As well as expertise from within the membership of the Review Group, contributions, evidence and comments were also received from the Bishop of Rochester, the Bishop of Worcester, the Bishop of Guildford, the House of Bishops' Theological Group, Professor Charles Handy, the Revd Dr Martin Davie, Theological Consultant to the House of Bishops, Dr Linda Woodhead of the University of Lancaster, Dr Al McFadyen of the University of Leeds and Canon Professor Anthony Thistleton, Professor of Christian Theology at the University of Nottingham. Particular thanks are due to the Revd Dr Malcolm Brown, Principal of the East Anglican Ministerial Training Course, who prepared a substantial discussion paper for the Group.
2. There is some detail contained within the *Didache* and the *Apostolic Constitutions*. For details of the situation in Rome and elsewhere see A.H.M. Jones, 'Church finance in the fifth and sixth Centuries', *Journal of Theological Studies*, n.s. 11 (1960), pp. 84–94, especially, p. 91ff. The Group is indebted to Professor David Wright of the University of Edinburgh for drawing attention to this reference.
3. R.T. France, *Matthew*, Tyndale New Testament Commentaries, IVP, pp. 179–80.
4. Leon Morris, *Luke*, Tyndale New Testament Commentaries, p. 199.
5. I.H. Marshall, *Luke*, New International Greek Testament Commentary, p. 421.
6. F.W. Gingrich and F.W. Danker, *Shorter Lexicon of the Greek New Testament*.
7. The LXX (the Septuagint) is the ancient Greek version of the Old Testament.
8. Gordon Fee, *The First Epistle to the Corinthians*, New International Commentary on the New Testament (Greek text), p. 409.
9. Fee, p. 413.
10. Leon Morris, *1 Corinthians*, Tyndale New Testament Commentaries, p. 133.
11. Morris, p. 131.
12. F.W. Gingrich and F.W. Danker, *Thayer's Greek Definitions*.
13. Fee, p. 399
14. Fee, pp. 413–4
15. Fee, p. 422.
16. The reference is from the NIV. KJV and NRSV follow the NIV by translating *time* as honour; REB translates as 'stipend'.
17. G.W. Knight, *The Pastoral Epistles: A Commentary on the Greek Text*, New International Greek Testament Commentary, pp. 231–2
18. Gingrich and Danker, *Thayer's Greek Definitions*.
19. Vincent's Word Studies, reprinted Wm. B. Eerdmans, 1957.

20. Knight, p.232; J.N.D. Kelly, *A Commentary on the Pastoral Epistles*, pp. 124–5; M. Dibelius and H. Conzelmann, *The Pastoral Epistles*; Donald Guthrie, *The Pastoral Epistles*, Tyndale New Testament Commentaries, pp. 117–18.
21. Knight, p. 235.
22. Guthrie, p. 118.
23. Details of the remuneration policies adopted by Tearfund are given in Appendix 3.

appendix 6

1. 'Guaranteed Annuities and Personal Grants' has been substituted for 'Benefice endowment income (including net glebe income)' which appeared in the method of computing income approved by the Synod in 1975.
2. 'Easter Offering' includes 'Whitsun Offering' where appropriate.
3. i.e. after allowing such expenses properly incurred in earning the income as may be agreed between the clergyman or woman and his or her diocese.

index

Note: Page numbers in italics refer to tables.

generosity and sacrifice

a summary of the report of the Clergy Stipends Review Group

This summary outlines the recommendations and supporting arguments from *Generosity and Sacrifice: The Report of the Clergy Stipends Review Group*. It will assist in the widespread debate in diocesan synods, Houses of Clergy and Laity and other groups.

Date of publication: November 2001
ISBN: 0-7151-2611-3
Approximate price: £3.95

generosity and sacrifice

the results of the clergy stipends survey

In 1999 the Archbishops' Council set up a working party under the chairmanship of the Ven. Dr John Marsh, Archdeacon of Blackburn, to conduct a review of clergy stipends, including the level at which they are set.

In order to find out how clergy are managing financially, the review group commissioned a survey of all the clergy and licensed lay workers who are listed on the Church Commissioners' payroll. Clergy and lay workers were asked both to provide information about their financial circumstances and to express their views about a number of issues which relate to their remuneration.

Nearly two-thirds of those who were sent the questionnaire replied, which shows how strongly people feel about their stipends and associated issues. The questions included the following:

- How many clergy own their own homes?
- How many clergy are in debt?
- What do clergy feel about higher stipends for bishops?
- Can parishes afford to pay their clergy more?
- What is clergy job satisfaction like?

This report gives the answers to these questions and many more.

ISBN: 0-7151-2602-4
Price: £8.95

Both these publications are available from Church House Bookshop (Tel: 020 7898 1300/02; Fax: 020 7898 1305; Order securely online: www.chbookshop.co.uk).